CW00530653

ONE-HORSE FARM

One-Horse Farm
CROFTING IN
THE WEST HIGHLANDS

by

Raymond O'Malley

With photographs by the Author

The Pentland Press
Edinburgh – Cambridge – Durham – USA

© Raymond O'Malley 1948, 1995

First published in 1948 by
Frederick Muller Ltd

This edition published in 1995 by
The Pentland Press
Hutton Close
South Church
Bishop Auckland
Durham

ISBN 1 85821 364 9
Printed and bound by Antony Rowe Ltd, Wiltshire

In memory of my wife

D.

" There is none worthy
Respecting her that's gone."

" But, chiefly, do not let us overestimate the importance of the economic problem, or sacrifice to its supposed necessities other matters of greater and more permanent significance. It should be a matter for specialists—like dentistry. If economists could manage to get themselves thought of as humble, competent people, on a level with dentists, that would be splendid ! "

LORD KEYNES, *Essays in Persuasion.*

Contents

ix

x CONTENTS

Illustrations

ILLUSTRATIONS

Foreword

My gratitude is due to Mr Colin Macdonald and to the Moray Press for permission to quote from "Highland Journey"; to Mr J. Middleton Murray for permission to use in Chapter VIII material that first appeared in "Adelphi"; and to Kodak Ltd. for a priority sale of films that made the illustrations possible. My debt to the crofters of Strath Ascaig must also be recorded here: its extent will be apparent from the text.

Introduction to the second edition by Owen Chadwick, former Master of Selwyn college, Cambridge

To be a teacher in South-West England and then throw it off perforce and become a crofter in Wester Ross may not be unique but the experience of Raymond O'Malley and his wife Dorothy produced a unique book. When the war against Hitler broke out he was on the staff at a school in Devon. On moral and religious grounds he was sure that it was wrong for him to fight. So he must appear before a tribunal, and then another tribunal, that dealt with conscientious objectors. The higher court gave the order that he could be exempt provided that he stopped teaching and worked on a farm. He bicycled the length of Britain looking for farms where he might work, and finally decided that it should be in Scottish crofts. For a year he learnt the trade as an employee of Scottish farmers, sometimes happily and sometimes unhappily. Then he and Dorothy put their money into renting the croft, Achbeg, not far from Kyle of Lochalsh and in a rough hidden valley from which the Cuillin mountains could often be seen in the distance. It was a brave act for they were not sure that they could do it with success. They might lose their savings. They could hardly expect Highlanders to welcome a 'foreigner' with open arms. They might expect that crofters whose sons were taken by the State to fight in France or Egypt, and some of whom never came back, could resent a stranger, young and fit, embusqué among the mountains. They knew that they were in for a hard way of life. This book is the story of what happened. But it is much more than that.

First, it is a rare description of a Highland way of life in a vanishing world: how to farm land where the sheep got lost in the mountain, and rain came down too often, and the cobbles which were the only cheap flooring (for they could be picked off the beach) were impossible to keep clean, and the midges were more prolific than in any other area of Britain, and the light in winter was not enough for all the jobs that needed light, and the paraffin lamps risked setting the straw alight, and the nearest vet was no nearer than the east coast of Scotland. And this pair go at it not with fear but in wonder. The book is full of air, pure and sweet to breathe, not only mountain and sea air, but the wind that freshens eyes to see enchantment wherever they look. It is full of moorland and bog and bracken and peat and storms and wispy clouds. It is the more charming because this is that unusual farmer, a student of English literature, who can write with simplicity and unpretentiousness and at times with beauty.

Next it is a study in humanity. The Highlanders who might have rejected them accepted them at once as two of themselves. Without that their life would hardly have been tolerable, for the neighbouring crofts depended on each other for help, expecially in crises where the labour of more than two was needed, like hauling out a cow stuck in a deep ditch. The title of *One-horse farm* does not mislead, for they must have a horse and could not afford two and the one horse could not be employed fully and had to turn an honest penny by carting coal. The author enjoyed the old Gaelic customs and meetings, and tried to learn Gaelic, and shared in whisky rituals though he evidently preferred to be more moderate in consumption than his male friends, for when a bottle was necessary at Hogmanay he had to get it out of England. He loved their dancing, and above all their folk-songs; and laments the decline of folk-songs not only in the Highlands but everywhere, not without an act of faith in their moral importance for the culture and well-being of communities. He enjoyed tramps and even drunks, but then he enjoyed humanity. He was amused at the need to haggle over prices and was disconsolate that he was incompetent and that he always ended by paying almost the price that was first asked. Nature is welcomed as compensation for the aching hours of labour—the seapinks and the loch, the briars and the heather and the bluebells, the souwester breeze upon his cheeks.

Then it is a study in affection for animals, especially the one horse and the few cows; the more numerous sheep are anonymous but still companions; the reader makes friends with Cheetah and Maundy the cows, and Prince the horse, and even some of the ewes and the lambs. We are as pained as the author when Maundy is last seen being driven too fast towards a slaughter-house. It cannot be called the love of all living creatures because there was never a fiercer indictment of the midge, which was as dangerous to the animals as pestilent to the humans, and he never succeeded in liking anything about the hens except eggs; he found hens brainless, 'their whole emotional range seems to run only from indignation to consternation'. But the affection for the larger animals, smiling and rueful, at times reminds the reader of James Herriot the vet on the Yorkshire moors; and with similar moments of crisis, like the attempt to help a disturbed cow in the dark and the sudden recognition that his stomach was perfectly sited for a thrust from the horn. He was fascinated by the cows, their skittishness and their solemnities, their sense of hierarchy, and how they made way for each other in going through a gate.

There are mysteries. Two of the photographs have telegraph poles which do not seem to go anywhere. He will tell us nothing of the Highlanders' religion though he approves their Sabbath and it is evident he knows a lot about it; and not far away was a church which could hold a thousand and was attended then by about a hundred. At one point he deliberately smashed six panes of glass in someone's window and as deliberately he will not tell us why. There is a person in the book who is of its essence and with just as hard a work to do, yet we learn hardly more of her than her name and her nursing of a sick cow and her sorting of potatoes; not because she was less than important to him but for the opposite reason, the memory is so sacred that he feels he cannot write about her. He leaves us wanting to know, but did something more moving: he dedicated the book to her memory.

There was a Gandhi in him; he disliked machines; he suspected the transistor of killing Gaelic tradition; resented it that he could not get his ploughing done in the time unless he joined the other crofts in hiring a travelling tractor; was vexed that he could not protect his crops from animals and at last was forced to ring the field with an electric fence. He went to a Gaelic funeral, and listened to the old Gaelic psalms, and found them haunting, and saw a heron watching from a distance, and revered the dignity of the mourners, and thought of the permanence of death and burial, and was sure that one day New York and London will have crumbled into the dust, and men and women would be buried with this quiet decency in which a whole community shared. Truly the book has not only a historical importance as a study of the past; not only a literary importance as a rare prose in a world where few writers have that experience; but also as a moral vision from a mind which reflected with a gentle wisdom on the earthiness of the world, during months when no day passed without horror in Europe as the continent sought to destroy itself for the second time within thirty years.

CHAPTER I

" No more school," Orlando said, and Grace was glad for she
believed in mice for cats, not Education.
                KATHLEEN HALE—*Orlando's Home Life.*

Ours really was a one-horse farm, too small to support
a pair of horses and yet unworkable without the one. With
its irregular, scattered patches of run-down soil, its hill of
bracken, peat and rock, remote from shops and markets,
at a high latitude and washed out by the West Highland
downpour, Achbeg was a farm economist's nightmare. We
scythed our corn and we threshed it with a stick. Much
of our haymaking was done indoors. There was no choice.
   The district does not take kindly to modern ways, for
many reasons. Great stretches of moorland and rock hold
apart the pockets and fringes of cultivation in the Highlands, and fingers of the sea probe deep into the land.
Owing to rock, bog and water the roads have always been
few and rough, suited in parts for pack-ponies at best.
Some townships must still be approached on foot or by
boat. It is the wildest, cleanest, perhaps the poorest corner
of Britain, and its beauty has been the setting of many
tragedies. A doctor's report was quoted in the Commons
not long ago. An acute surgical case had to be taken from
a village to hospital. A northerly gale blowing straight
on to the beach prevented the removal of the patient from
her home on the first day. The next day was almost as
bad. Villagers carried the patient on a stretcher to another
beach, where it was placed in a rowing boat and taken out
to a larger fishing boat. Owing to the gale and the high
sea, the patient was taken on board with the greatest
difficulty. An hour and a half later she was transferred
with equal difficulty to a rowing boat, from that to the

I

beach, and taken along the beach on a stretcher to a car for the 85-mile journey to hospital. Her feelings may be imagined. " In a similar case the patient died."

Such calamities must have been common before the railway edged into this wilderness two generations ago. It crept over the dead ground at the watershed and down to Stromeferry, on a finger of the western sea. For better or for worse it began to drain away old customs and old ideas and to infuse new ones. It had more strength to change the countryside than had Prince Charlie, more even than the sheep and the deer. And it was built with a State subsidy.

There are still marks of Strome's brief glory : the barred window of the former police cell, the sleeping lighthouse that guided the Stornoway boat through the rocks and currents, and the stump of the pier from which rang the cries of the fishermen, that still echo in the minds of living people. A grateful company built six houses for its surfacemen at the foot of a cavernous north slope, where the sun cranes down in summer. Soon the railway drove on to Kyle of Lochalsh. Maps continue to give Stromeferry a typographical importance that is belied by the reality, a handful of cottages hemmed between loch and hill.

From the ferry and the station a road runs up a steep hill, by a quaking causeway across some bog, and down into Strath Ascaig. We knew it as " The Strath " or " The Glen," and the hill as " The Brae," just as earlier men gave the uniqueness of " Ouse " and " Avon " to their own particular river. In the middle of the Strath, which is a mere cleft in the hills, lies Achbeg.

Long ago a great slab of rock must have sunk a thousand feet to form our Glen ; to a geologist, a very small fault, but impressive enough as you gaze up at the twin rocks of Fernaig and Portachullin, where they straddle the sea end of the Glen. The house of Achbeg stands on a line of rock that dams the Glen mid-way. Our front windows, looking east, showed the boggy flats set in an amphitheatre of planted conifers ; on misty mornings

The Glén. Its green fields are encircled by the Forestry conifers and the higher hills rising to Ben Killilan.

Portachullin Hill. Loch Carron winds far inland; and nearer, the raised beach supports old peat workings.

Highland shepherd. Tom's whole life has been devoted to sheep-work, and his opinions are highly valued.

The author. Hay for winter milk.

or by moonlight one could easily imagine that a mile or two of water still lay between us and the pair of white cottages at the head of the Glen. There were arable fields within the horse-shoe of larch and fir, forming several crofts and a couple of farms ; and above the tree-level rough grazing rolled away to the real mountains.

From the rock in the steading we could look down the Glen across Fernaig, the next farm, to a glimpse of Loch Carron, Raasay and the Applecross Hills. Curtains of grey rain and mist often glided upon us from Applecross, blotting out the islands, the lighthouse, the strange bog on the raised beach, our own small fields, and at length the rock itself. After sunset Applecross was a flat wall of indigo blue ; at dawn it was often pink. It could be gnarled and brown, or smooth and grey. In snow it had blue valleys not noticed before. Lines of ruby fire smouldered across its blackness in early spring, when heather burning must go on despite the war-time curfew. In all its moods Applecross was remote and austere, yet it had the kindness of a sheltering wall.

Creag Mhaol, our own hill, despite its cliffs, showed a smooth silhouette against the flicker of the Northern Lights, in contrast to the volcanic cone of Meallan. From our garden I often watched the shower of sparks from the imagined crater of Meallan as the Pleiades rose of a frosty evening. At the foot of Meallan lay Achmore, the farm of our neighbour Donald. Achmore and Achbeg, the Big Field and the Little Field. There was never a better neighbour than Donald and we ran the two farms almost as one. It was a lop-sided partnership—just how lop-sided will appear later—for I was neither a farmer nor a Highlander. By training and vocation I am a schoolmaster. Both my wife D. and I had a general interest in farming : we liked to watch the changing colours and textures of the Devon fields in their dark unchanging framework of banks ; to hear the first lambs and the hesitant whine of the thresher : at times, to lend a hand. We had the townsman's patter on farming policy. But of farming as part of the world's

A

work, the why and wherefore of it all, we had very little understanding. Some day, we told ourselves, we would take a small farm, perhaps a market garden, perhaps a croft; but the reasons for staying in our chosen groove were strong and it would have taken a considerable jolt to get us out of it.

The jolt came, with the War. We had long before decided that we could take no direct part in any war, and the considerations that had led us to become pacifists seemed to be as valid after 1939 as before. A sympathetic Local Tribunal permitted me to go on with my teaching. For reasons that do not matter here I appealed to London, where the conditions of my military exemption were altered to exclude teaching and include farming—a puzzling decision. The members of the Appeal Tribunal were no doubt doing their best at an impossible task, and I trust that each of them, when summoned before a higher Tribunal, will receive at least as fair a hearing. Furthermore, I hope he will find that any documents permitted and submitted on that dread occasion will have been read.

Farming, then, it was to be, and the question was, where. We decided to make this the occasion for a thorough break: we would go either to a district of highly mechanised farming that anticipated the immediate future, or to a district that had resisted change and might tell us something of the past.

I set off, therefore, on a cycling tour of exploration, making the longer hops by train. In Norfolk I learned little that helped, because heavy snow fell. The red-brick farmhouses glowed brilliantly in the cold sunlight, but field-work was at a standstill. At one place I saw men shovelling beet. As fast as they filled the one lorry another took its place. The men were never idle and their backs never straight. I learned a little.

In the Lakes I met an old farmer who told me farming was a mug's game. He was putting all his money into shipping: the returns were good and the Government insurance covered all risks.

" If you were a boy again," I asked, " would you go to sea ? "

He saw the catch and smiled.

" No, I suppose I'd farm again."

Encouraged, I went on with my exploring.

If I liked the hummocky Lakeland hills, where you are always peering down somebody's chimney, and where you wonder how the snowdrifts fail to engulf the valley farm-houses altogether, I was entirely captivated by the High-lands. From the first day I felt at home there.

It was partly the scenery—the storm and stress of the hills plunging into the composure of the sea lochs. Some-times old earth boundaries wrinkled the slopes like the veins of a clenched fist. Along some chance contour, impartial as a snowline, scattered wisps of cloud marked out the big hills from the small ; then perhaps a heavy grey ceiling would span the glens ; and then again mottled shadows would scud at tortoise pace over land and water. Snow fell here too. Seen from a porthole, Castlebay was scratchy black and white, like an etching, but animated by moving dots. Our boat had brought in the bread after Barra had been storm-bound, and on every track children and old people were hurrying to the warmth of little cottages, loaf under arm. Then there were the sickle bays of pure shell-sand on the Atlantic coast of the Isles, blind-ing white even in the subdued light of mid-winter. Many of the cottages had walls a yard thick and a hump of heather thatch. When searching winds pelted in from St. Kilda they stood warm, ship-shape and comfortable, and as firm as a cave. With some other men I crossed the Benbecula ford in a dung-cart. After the roughness of the Minch, in the early morning light, the houses jogging toward us on the water had the over-sharpness of dream pictures. The brisk wind stirred my senses to reality. It was clean, and right. (After the Outer Isles most of Eng-land has a suburban air.) We passed men and women who were paddling across the ford. It is safe enough for those who know the way ; but there are many sad stories of those who were mistaken, and those who lingered just too long at the inn, to be swept off by the racing tide.

Partly it was the country; but much more it was the people. That they were poor was plain enough, but whatever they had to eat they offered. As I had no Gaelic, they spoke in English—a very beautiful, deliberate English coloured with translations of Gaelic idioms, in no way resembling broad Scots. One very old woman told me of Scotland's troubles—the evictions, the coming of the sheep and then the deer, and the emigration of men driven to desperation. The poetry of her words was no mere trick of an unfamiliar idiom. Though the people worked hard they had always leisure to talk. A man who had been preparing lazy-beds came and talked, until the tide had risen for a boat. Above all I liked them for being themselves. Earlier, as I had come out of the station in one of the Scottish cities, I had encountered a vision in black, tripping daintily across the tram-lines in the best Hollywood manner, a perfect replica of the momentary feminine ideal, and dragging a small afterthought of an infant; but here in the islands and the glens of the mountains there were no baby Garbos. The men and women were too much absorbed in their world of family, croft and boat to act a part. In their welcome there was neither servility nor faked cordiality. I fell in with some commercial travellers who knew the whole district intimately. They told me many tales of religious customs surviving on the smaller islands, of boats, fishing, lobsters, cattle, crops, seaweed, births, marriages and deaths; they spoke of much that I could not repeat here, but they spoke without prurience. And I met a man who could quote most of Burns, and did so, and who knew the ways of every beast and insect. And a seaman who had the manner that seamen have, and shepherds, and others who must be alone for long periods.

And I learned with astonishment the Scotch way with whisky. Four of us had called at a small inn after crossing a ferry. Four pints of beer were placed on the counter, and beside each a smaller and fiercer drink. Four right hands seized the four small glasses (my own lagging a little as I followed the lead) ; a very Gaelic sound— " slainte "—was uttered ; a flick of the wrist accompanied a smart jerk of the head, with a synchronisation plainly achieved by long practice ; and that was all. The beer followed at leisure. When my turn came I placed down a ten-shilling-note, and the change was hardly worth lifting ; two of my companions were crofters. I marvelled at this strange ritual, and to-day, years later, I still marvel. Ten-shilling-notes do not grow readily on heather moors.

Back in Devon I described my trip to D. and we made the decision that took us, first to the Outer Isles, and eventually to our own small farm of Achbeg. We knew that to a sentimentalist it would seem the wrong choice— the hankering after a picturesque past rather than an adventurous zest for the future ; but we were satisfied that it was the right choice.

There were two main reasons for our decision, but before giving them I must say that we were aware of one obvious objection that might be raised. Official policy was (naturally) to grow as much food as possible within the country. A worker on a fertile, mechanised farm adds more to the country's larder than a man on marginal ground. Since, however, all ground was to be worked, including the marginal, it was actually better for an unskilled man to go to the poorer, less productive ground, and release a better man for the better ground. This by the way.

Our first reason was one about which I have since become much clearer thanks to an article published by Dr. Hugh H. Bennett in the Journal of the Ministry of Agriculture for November, 1943, and subsequent private correspondence. Dr. Bennett was Chief of the United States Soil Conservation Service. If his facts are correct, then the problem he poses is about the most important in the world, hardly less important (though less urgent) than the control of atomic energy. I have never seen his facts confirmed, or challenged.

His first fact is that the cultivable land of the globe works out at only two acres per person—four billion acres for two billion people. This represents only 11 per cent. of the land surface of the globe, the rest being mountains, deserts and other land that cannot be cultivated in any foreseeable time. The estimate is no irresponsible guess, but the outcome of careful research by Dr. Bennett's staff, based on the best available figures. Two acres, it must be remembered, not of good land, but of land ranging from the best down to the very poorest that can be cultivated at all.

His second fact is that two acres of such land will not provide an adequate diet for one person ; " it is barely enough to supply a minimum diet."

What bearing have these facts, supposing them to be facts, on this question of " yesterday " and " to-morrow " ? They make it very much harder to be sure which *is* the farming of to-morrow ; they even suggest that large-scale mechanised farming *may* prove to have been after all a momentary aberration of history.

Consider for a moment the effect of machinery. A machine that trebles the amount a man can do trebles the wealth he can produce—provided there is no other limiting factor. In some cases there is no further limiting factor ; so far as I am aware, the only limit to the number of wrist-watches we may possess is set by our skill in devising effortless means of manufacturing them. With food it is otherwise. Assuming Dr. Bennett to be right, and taking the world as a unit, we must conclude that what matters is not the amount of food that can be squeezed out of a day's work, but the amount that can be coaxed out of an acre of ground. Acres are short, hands are abundant— that (or more strictly the abundance of mouths) is the whole problem. Where machinery saves both labour and land, fine—let us have it. There are such cases—on steep hill-sides, and in the reclamation of wet ground for instance. But where machinery saves labour at the expense of acres,

then in the end it will have to go. On the whole, that is
the effect of extensive farming. Given equal skill, equally
good seed, and (in general terms) equal access to the results
of research, the small-scale intensive farmer can get more
food from his acres than can the more typically " modern "
farmer. True, the Americans (like the British themselves,
whose food comes from sparsely populated dominions) can
grow their own food by extensive methods and yet enjoy
a very high standard of living, but that is because they have
more than their share of acres. If Indians and Chinese
poured into America until the density of population were
levelled out, or if the Americans felt a sudden urge to
share freely with the Indians and Chinese the produce of
their extra acres (a most improbable urge), then the situation would be very different. The Americans too would
be concerned above all with output per acre, not output
per hour. Some day the democratic notion may prevail
that the individual members of the human race all have
equal claim upon the most precious of the world's resources ; and if that day comes the crofter and the despised
peasant farmer may come back into their own : a new type
of crofter and peasant, no doubt, but one having more in
common with the crofter and peasant of to-day than with
the paid factory-hand of to-day.

The powers of industrialisation are greatly over-rated.
Possibly we shall in the end persuade the inhabitants of
Mars to grow our food for us, in return for imports of
toothpaste, cameras and other manufactured goods ; or we
may learn to grow crops several layers deep, or to by-pass
agriculture altogether, making food direct from sunlight
or other energy ; but all of these possibilities are remote.
In the meantime the shortage of acres is the world's chief
problem ; and industrialisation must be content to multiply
all of our forms of wealth *except* that which matters most.
We shall starve in the midst of plenty—plenty of manufactured goods. By " we " I mean, of course, the human
race : *some* of us may continue to avoid under-nourishment.

We were not unduly bothered, therefore, at the prospective charge of turning our backs on the future, being by no means convinced that current trends in farming had any considerable future.

Our second reason was our belief that those relics of the farming past that have survived have far more to teach the present than the present shows any sign of wishing to learn. On this, too, we have since become much clearer. What has made us clearer is the experience to be recorded in the present book, and a fuller consideration will therefore come more properly in the concluding chapter. Here a brief note only is required.

Living and earning a living have come to be thought of as unrelated, even contrary, concerns. " Are you waiting for the foreman ? " I asked some acquaintances who were standing around. " No," came the answer, " we're waiting for five o'clock." Out of that " waiting for five o'clock " have grown both the material affluence and the spiritual desolation of the West. It is (we believed, D. and I) a paralysing divorce. A former age—of which peasant culture to-day is a relic—held that the function of the good society was to reconcile the two interests, so that in the pursuit of economic ends men achieved a spiritual (or, if you so prefer it, a moral or aesthetic) goal. A later age considered it a foolish heresy—and built the mining towns. Now we are not so sure after all. There is a passage in Lord Keynes's " General Theory " which reads : " I was brought up to believe that the attitude of the Medieval Church to the rate of interest was inherently absurd, and that the subtle discussions aimed at distinguishing the return on money-loans from the return to active investment were merely jesuitical attempts to find a practical escape from a foolish theory. But I now read these discussions as an honest intellectual effort to keep separate what the classical theory has inextricably confused together, namely, the rate of interest and the marginal efficiency of capital." Nobody who has followed Keynes's analysis will suppose the consequences of the confusion to have been merely theoretical.

D. and I had often felt instinctively at one with peasants we knew on the continent, and now again I had the same feeling in the Highlands. We do not imagine, of course, that the advances of the last century or so have been solely material; there is much that is new in the intellectual and spiritual spheres that is exceedingly precious. None the less, we knew that the people in the Highlands could teach us something that cannot be learned in the dormitory suburbs of our great cities, however prosperous, nor even in agricultural districts that are economically and socially dependent on the towns. We chose, therefore, the Highlands.

A year later, on the May Term, we took a croft of our own, which was Achbeg. May Term (28th May) is a great day in the Scottish farming world. Throughout the country on that day, carts are being piled high with personal belongings, cattle are being driven through unaccustomed gateways, ploughmen are sizing up their new employers, and farmers their new farms. It is the day of agricultural general post, from which most contracts and leases date. And at twelve o'clock precisely on that day, in 1943, we became tenants of Achbeg and owners of a flock of mountain sheep. The exact minute of the transfer is fixed by custom. It might matter. Sheep have a way of gathering under trees in a storm, and the responsibility for a loss of hundreds of pounds might depend upon the timing of a lightning flash.

CHAPTER II

THREE PUN' A WEEK

" The story of my life
And the particular accidents gone by
Since I came to this isle."
SHAKESPEARE—" The Tempest."

We had been in Scotland for a year before taking a croft of our own. It was an absorbing year. How little we knew about the work and how much therefore we owed to the neighbours who helped us so unsparingly, may, in passing, become plain from a note of the year's apprenticeship.

To obtain paid farm-work in the Highlands (or Islands) was not easy; crofts and farms are too small to support paid labour and are worked by father and mother, sons and daughters. The few paid men are usually shepherds or other skilled men competent to take full responsibility. By good luck (helped very little by the Military Permit authorities, for this was a Protected Area), we had the choice of two jobs and went to the Outer Isles.

The Outer Hebrides are not the icy, leaden-skied region that Southerners imagine. They are fairly flat. The Atlantic winds must pass over the islands and over the Minch before they meet mountains of any size. Accordingly our Island was sunny, no wetter than most of Devon, and, thanks to the Gulf Stream, no colder in winter; but the wind rarely ceases. Occasional tornadoes lift whole haystacks, and the heavy stones on ropes round the eaves of the houses are there for a purpose.

We were greatly interested in the life and work of our district. On the Island many of the crofts or smallholdings are of reasonable size, having been created for Servicemen returning after the first World War. While the newer houses, built with Government aid, have not the tremendous solidity of the older ones, they have many added amenities, and allow the great boon of privacy within the family. Often the present barn was formerly the dwelling house, perhaps a but and ben—two rooms, one " but " and the other " ben " : without and within. Cattle had sometimes occupied one end and the family the other. As there are no real trees in the whole of Long Island, the roof-timbers had been ferried over from the mainland.

To a considerable extent the crofters live off their own produce, but money plays an increasing part in their economy. To the mainland go calves, sheep, wool, and the very hardy Highland ponies or a heavier cross. It is no uncommon event to see a foal trotting happily on the roads, circling its mother who is harnessed in trap or cart. Eggs and tweed also cross the Minch, and occasionally an allowance from sons and daughters on the mainland helps to balance the family budget. When children become ministers of religion, doctors or nurses, as a surprising number do, they remain proud of their origin, and spend many holidays helping on the croft. It is not easy to make what is nowadays considered a living off 12 or even 18 acres with a share of rough grazing ; some of the men therefore go away for spells of work elsewhere. There was formerly an ingenious plan called working for stamps : MacA. employed MacB. for the requisite time and MacB. then employed MacA. The wages cancelled out—but both MacA. and MacB. were now eligible for unemployment insurance pay ! On a small island near the main island there were two families only. We were often told that the head of one was part-time minister, the head of the other part-time postman, but I never tried to verify this. Trawlers and other influences have practically killed the fishing here.

As in the middle ages, and for the same reason, the ground comprising each croft is in a number of scattered strips, some near the house, some on the more peaty ground, and some down on the machair. The machair is the long strip of excellent soil along the Atlantic dunes, so sandy that one would never expect the good crops of corn that it bears. It must be one of the few parts of the Highlands that have enough lime, powdered coral from the beaches being carried in by the high winds. So far as possible the corn strips are grouped together, in order that a single round of rabbit netting may protect them all. Rabbits abound ; on a warm evening they bask in overlapping family parties, like the trippers on Brighton beach.

For certain purposes the crofts are grouped in townships, and the responsibility for the maintenance of communal roads and drains lies with the Township Committee. As there are few fences, horses and rams are tethered, and a boy or an old man is employed to herd all the cattle of the township together by the shore, or up in the hills, or, in winter, on the strips also. For all grazing is shared from a certain date onwards, by which time crops must have been lifted. In spite of its advantages, the system of shared grazing discourages individual enterprise. If any one crofter wished to experiment with improved grasses, all would share the gain though he alone would bear the cost. The better, closer peat hags have been worked out during earlier centuries ; now the families must bring their peat long distances, or be content with inferior fuel. A large stack of peat is built by the gable of every cottage, as large and neat as the hull of an inverted smack.

It was plain that I had much to learn before we could set up on our own. Given time enough, and an accommodating cow, I could milk : that acquirement and reasonable health were my only qualifications. A crofter showed me how to dress a horse. I was greatly interested by the neat ingenuity of the harness, and he, I believe, found equal interest in the discovery of a man who could not dress a horse. But like all the Islanders he showed perfect politeness. My work was partly on a ramshackle home farm and partly in a high-walled garden. I made all the mistakes. My greatest trial was a senile horse who held me in the frankest contempt. Sometimes he would not budge for me at all ; at best he would break into a brisk crawl. Just once, for a couple of seconds, I stirred him into the semblance of a bucking bronco, and that by oversight : I couped (tipped) the cart without unhitching the reins from the frame. A few highlights stand out in my memory of the summer's work. We were trying one breezy day to gather hay on an exposed field when the wind rolled the whole crop into a monstrous sausage against the dyke. Later we dragged a dead cow over the sands to the recognised burial-place. Nick, the horse, set a funeral pace. By chance the herd noticed us, and all the 70 or 80 cattle in the township fell in as mourners, a few of them trumpeting their grief.

Here I did learn something about the general crofting economy. The job, however, was not a success, for personal reasons. The full story must wait : when porridge had been scattered over the fireplace, vegetables (pot and all) flung out of the window, and six contiguous panes of glass deliberately smashed by me, we felt it was time to move on. There was a good croft vacant nearby, the house of which stood on a rock by the shore. " Look," said the owner (strictly, he owned only the house and other " improvements," not the ground itself), " you could put the pan on the fire in the morning, slip to the end of the house with a rod, and be back with a pair of cuddies for your breakfast before the fat was fit to take them." But there is a great demand for crofts on the islands. When we found that the Township wanted it kept for the Islanders who would later be returning, we withdrew our application.

While waiting for a more permanent place on the west again, I took several temporary jobs on the east. Dialect for the first time became our problem. In the Fifeshire region most consonants are a variant of the guttural stop, and most vowels a uniform short " u " as in " jug." Or so it seemed to my English ears. After receiving orders I would sit under a hedge and puzzle out : should I harness the horses or water the bull ? Of course I'm not complaining—I was there from choice; but it was an added reason for returning west.

Some friends took me to meet a Mr. Hardie, who was scything a track round a crop. From barley the crop graded off into pure spurrey, and we made the mistake of taking a short cut through the weeds.

" I would have thought you'd know better than that," he said.

" I'm sorry—we thought it was waste ground. I hear you've a job."

" It's only temporary, mind. Over the harvest."

" That's all I want."

" What about wages ? "

" What do you suggest ? "

" Three pun' a week."

" Right."

" When will you start ? "

" To-morrow."

" Seven o'clock. Do you want the house ? "

" What house ? "

" By the road there. It goes with the job. You can have it if you want it."

" What rent ? "

" No rent. It's only temporary, mind. I can't pay a man after the tatty-hooking."

So I became " Mr. Hardie's man " over the harvest. All our communications were made in that staccato manner, though I've left out the dialect. He always pushed the three bank-notes into my hand and bolted indoors. He punched the horses on the nose with all his strength if they misbehaved ; and while he urged the binder round and round the barley-field, his left leg swinging inert like the tail of a stage monkey, his voice roared to the horses a steadily reiterated : " Erch, ye bounders, erch, ye bounders . . ." The actual word had more colloquial force than " bounders," but I never once heard it used when the land-girl was within sight (though she must needs have gone far afield to be beyond hearing !).

That barley-crop gave much trouble. To begin with, the ancient binder would not cut up the slope, or with the wind, and had half-a-dozen mechanical whims, each of which required the attendance of a panting, poking human. Whenever the blade jammed the whole contingent of us pitched into the machine. Barley is always ticklish stuff to handle; the little saw-toothed points (called "barley oils" in Devon) have a painful knack of spontaneous travel, and parts of this field, in addition to the spurrey, had more thistles than barley. But we cut the crop and stooked it; and a gale demolished the stooks, and rain soaked the sheaves, and I spent the longest, wettest Sunday of my life restoring order. Next came the oats, or whatever the rooks had left of them, for they were over-ripe. I have never seen such congregations of rooks: when I think of the valley I still hear their metallic clamour. Our hours of work touched 70, but it was good to be getting in the corn, and I had formed a liking for Mr. Hardie. The land-girl worked longer than anyone: if Katie was typical, the W.L.A. deserves all praise.

There were also a couple of days of threshing, first at a neighbour's farm and then at our own. The whole orderly convulsion was directed by two black demons, wearing goggles, and wonderfully dignified, high on the platform. My own work was to remove the bundled straw that piled up at the tail. When the journey was short all was well, but when the straw-stack was farther away I could hardly keep pace with the machine and experienced the misery of working just beyond one's strength. Endless minutes would crawl by; then the mighty drone of the machine would falter and trail below audibility, the flapping belts came to rest, dust settled, the birds sang, and we all flung ourselves in the straw. Unlimited food and drink went round, until at a rising moan from the machine we all jumped back to our stations.

Owing to bad weather all work was behind schedule that year. Potato-lifting had barely begun when, in early November, we again went west. This time it was to the

Point of Knap, within sight of the Mull of Kintyre. Islay and Jura lay just across the water, and on clear days Rathlin and the Mountain of Mourne could just be made out.

First then there were the potatoes to be lifted. Some of the fields ran almost to the lines of seaweed on the shore. It was broken weather. Small storms came over the mountains of Jura, whipped up the sea as they advanced upon us, and passed on inland, leaving the exposed tubers bare and shining under the steaming horses. When the ground became too boggy we stopped for the day, but owing to the lateness of the season we carried on whenever possible. William, the shepherd, watched the muddy potatoes piled high in the stable. "Never more than three feet high in the west," he warned our employer, "they'll surely heat"; but in they all went, to a depth of five feet or so. Then we went on to another farm along the shore. I noticed the floats of a net drift by on the ebb as we started, and as we trudged back for tea the flow carried them in again. We had passed through all the stages of back-ache and enjoyed the later days of potato lifting.

Though I knew nothing of cattle and could not plough, I was now instated as ploughman-cattleman. My day, without being unduly long, started and ended in darkness. The three horses, and about 20 in-wintered cattle, were foddered before breakfast, the horses were groomed, and the stable was cleaned out. After breakfast came the routine of mashing turnips, feeding concentrates, mucking-out, putting out cattle, the spreading of clean bedding, and preparation of evening fodder and concentrates—all the usual routine of cattle-tending in winter. The rest of the day was spent on outside work of one kind and another. Sometimes the shepherd would need a hand with the sheep. He was an interesting man, William, with endless stories of sheep, and he liked to laugh. We watched aeroplanes flying low over the ancient churchyard one morning. "If the old people there could pop their heads out, wouldn't they just pull them back in again fast, now," he ruminated. We were forever dosing sheep with carbon

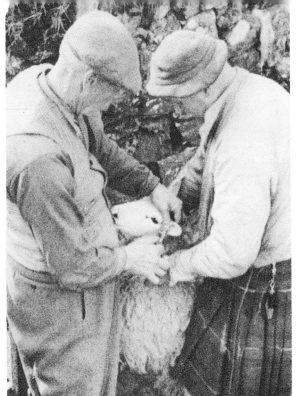

Earmarking hoggs. When she returns from wintering, each hogg is given her age-mark.

A sick lamb. Its mother had not enough milk.

The middle of the Glen. The Achbeg hill-ground rises beyond the cluster of buildings.

The higher hills. Across Glen Udalein to Ben Killilan and The Five Sisters.

tetrachloride pills, the wet ground being infested with liver-fluke. One of my tasks was to feed the tups (rams) daily, a dozen burly Blackface fellows with massive curled horns, and one very superior Border Leicester with none at all. I wish I could record that unilateral disarmament induced any change of heart on either side, but the Border Leicester's forehead was never without a scar.

For a while our field work was the reclaiming of some land that had gone back to marsh. I was astonished at the efficacy of field drains. On one day we would trace out the blocked tiles by means of " speers," pointed metal sticks ; we dug down here and there, ran a wire through the tile, and set the water running. We might have to stand on boards in order to get any footing at all. Next day there would be fairly firm ground and within a week large cracks appeared. I was told that some of the greenest fields about had quite recently been restored in this way from a waste of rushes.

William was right about the potatoes. The mud, dampness, lack of ventilation and proximity of the horses were together too much for them. Before anyone realised, the rot had extended throughout the pile. Most melted into a paste in which the remainder were suspended, and I was set to rescue the survivors. After expending much labour on labour-saving contraptions I found that there was nothing for it but to squelch my way through by handfuls. Doubtless the reader is familiar with the smell of a bad potato ; he is invited to conjure up the smell of a hundred thousand.

Several tramps used to call at the farm, among them one called Spoons because of the music he could draw from those instruments. He claimed to be the only man in Scotland, perhaps in the world, who could play a mouth-organ and two pairs of spoons at one time, and was longing for the war to end because the only decent mouth-organs were of German make. He would sometimes arrive unannounced, ask if there was work to be had, build himself a tent of sacks in the barn, and join

B

in the season's work at an agreed wage. He helped with the carting and spreading of the dung that spring, and with the draining. Early undernourishment had so shortened his bones that he had the air always of standing in a hole, but he was strong and a good worker. Then one morning the urge to move would come upon him. He would stuff all his belongings into a sack and be off at dawn without a word, perhaps to wander, perhaps for a spell in a big town. The money saved during months of hard work would be scattered in a few weeks of high living; then back he would go to his wandering and his casual jobs. Spoons, with his tent, his " buiks," and his habit of undressing at night " to let out the cold," was a cut above the ordinary tramp, but there are many of these wanderers, with no ties of home or family, each following his beat on the loneliest tracks of Lorne, Knapdale, and Kintyre, and in the remoter parts of the Highlands too. Sometimes they die, unmourned and unmissed, in cave or cairn among the rocks. Their life is bleak and even sordid, but it will be a sad day when there is not one tramp, tinker or gypsy left who will refuse to put his mark on the dotted line. If these words should ever catch his eye, I hope that Spoons will forgive me the publicity of print and drink a glass to our health at Hogmanay.

When I took the letters to the post of a morning, the beacon lights were still blinking along the Sound of Jura, and often the setting moon caught the snows of Islay, Jura and the smaller islands. This dream world would slowly fade into the light of common day, yet every night the magic was renewed. In an old church are housed medieval carvings every line of which is strong and alive, but they serve only to point a contrast. Knapdale is now dead. It is within the penumbra of the Lowland cities, and is sensibly awaiting the arrival of the week-ender.

This job, too, was a failure. My employer, a custard-powder manufacturer, held that I had not the outlook proper to a farm-servant, and it may well be imagined that my work was poor value for money when a skilled man could claim no more. Just at this moment came a letter out of the blue, when we were most in need of a friend. A little farm called Achbeg was to let. The advertisement spoke of 19 acres of arable and 193 of rough grazing; a tied flock of about 100 Cheviot sheep; good buildings—even a bath and hot water; and all this in the very district that had for us the strongest interest. My employer gave me leave to make a visit without loss of pay, and I liked Achbeg at once. My coat dragged heavily in the soft, almost imperceptible rain—I had no illusions about the climate. The hill ground was poor-to-average, even to my beginner's eyes, but I felt that the parks had possibilities. There were four of them near the steading, with the dark wavering line of alders marking the Ascaig, which was our march; and farther off, below the Falls where the stream frothed noisily in its gorge, there were four others. They needed liming, in places the drains had gone, and I could have wished they were less scattered, but they seemed workable enough. The buildings were good, slate and stone, the house compact, the barn airy and the byre-and-stable block well sited against the west gales. The fences I thought reasonably stock-proof (little did I know the Achbeg sheep!). It was about as large a farm as one couple could work in the conditions, and the Glen—who that loved Scotland could fail to love this green bay amongst the great poised waves of the hills?

I liked Achbeg, the expected rent seemed fair, and I felt there must be some sort of living in it, but what worried me was my utter incompetence. I barely knew a Galloway from a Poll Angus, and as for the Cheviots, I had thought they were park sheep pure and simple. Only now did I discover that the huge Cheviots of the down-Country farms had smaller, hardier cousins on the hills. And I could not even plough. To take Achbeg would be to throw away our capital, unless we had good neighbours. In this we were truly fortunate, and it was especially the candour of Donald's advice that swayed me.

I felt confident that we should work well together, and already I sensed, what I later found to be true, that there was in this Glen a quite exceptional spirit of co-operation. We put in a bid, and, after weeks of anxious waiting, were accepted as tenants. We parted from our employer, without rancour and without reluctance, and Spoons took my place. But we noticed the job in a Situations Vacant column a little later. No Defence Regulation could tie down Spoons.

So I ceased to be a paid man and set up as an independent crofter. As a paid man on several farms, I had learned only a little about farm work and management, but about one thing I had learned much—about current social assumptions. A salary-earner regards his work as a contract, binding on both parties, and made for their mutual advantage. On the whole he knows his legal and moral rights, and is accustomed to speak his mind without thought for consequences. Like many others who passed from the position of salary-earner to that of wage-earner, I found that I had formerly enjoyed unnoticed privileges. My employer was right: a certain outlook *is* thought proper to farm-servants and others of like standing. The demeanour of a policeman varies according to the cut of your clothing. Countless small humiliations and oppressions are inflicted upon those who can be relied upon to submit to them. But the experience is too common to need substantiation here with a catalogue of personal grievances.

The period of waiting to enter Achbeg was spent partly at a farm on the west coast of Inverness-shire. Not even the smaller islands have resisted change so much as this area, which is still Catholic, and farms not only without tractors but without horses. The " ploughing " is done with the spade. As many persons as can be collected stand in a straight line, 2 or 3 feet apart, each holding a spade. They score the turf lightly in front of them, dig in their spades, and at a given signal all together press. The whole furrow rolls over bodily. The next furrow is rolled into the trench thus created and so on. It is slow and laborious compared with ordinary ploughing, but gives a deeper tilth and (I imagine) a heavier crop. The surface drains would have to be buried before much use could be made of horses. We did hear of one piece of horse-ploughing, in which horses, plough and man leaped across the ditches in a wild blend of farming and steeple-chasing, but I do not know whether the experiment was repeated. Grass is top-dressed with seaweed carried from the shore in creels, and in creels also the peat is brought from distant moors by paths that are in places a mere ledge on a cliff. The wind here caught in a young woman's creel and swung her completely round, but she kept her footing. Bags of oatmeal weighing 10 stone were formerly carried by the women over the foot-track to the nearest harbour, several miles away, and coffins were carried for burial by the same path. The institution of the Ceilidh and the old Gaelic music are still thoroughly alive here. English is spoken only for foreigners. Calves and stirks were being groomed for the local sale. When the day came a procession of humans and haltered cattle went over the hill track. At dusk the humans alone returned, smiling readily: prices had been the best in living memory.

At last, a little before Term, we collected scraps of furniture and implements and tools, and moved into the Glen.

All this was several years ago now. Friends on both sides of the Border have urged us to write about our life in the north, but I make the attempt with some misgiving. Farming writers and other who describe their own experiences often show an alarming blind patch. There are passages in many books, well known and otherwise, that would be blameless if the beings described in them were the inhabitants of a public aquarium, but which become acutely embarrassing if the reader reflects that they are the inhabitants of some quiet farming valley, going their harmless ways, and fairly certain to read and discuss the book themselves. Even favourable comment must occa-

sion some awkwardness; indulgent humour or condescension ought to be unthinkable.

A hiker spent the night in our barn. For all I know
he may have been the great MacScribble, author of " Scent
o' Heather," and I may find myself anatomised in his next
little volume, " Smell o' Bog Myrtle " :—

" About nine I went along to hear the news, but as
I had half expected my host had no set. A typical Norse-
man, bowed from his years at the plough-handle, and
gaunt from the struggle with a stony soil, he put a good
face on it, remarking quaintly : ' We sold the thing
because we couldn't stand the drivel that came out of it.'
I sensed a character at once, and settled down to a hearty
chat."

That would be a poor return for the hospitality of our
kitchen. To the people of the Glen we owe far more than
a night's entertainment. Though we were strangers, alien
to their ways and indeed to their very language, the merest
novice at farming, and moreover pacifists at a time when
many faces were absent from their tables, they at once took
us into their community. They harvested our corn, lifted
our " tatties," and helped us in all our difficulties. This
book is the only thanks I can offer to those who were
our neighbours and will always be our friends. It is written
in the hope that, here and there, a reader who might have
gone to teach will stay to learn.

CHAPTER III

SHEEP—SUMMER

" Mountain ewes is a queer breed, Nora Burke, and I not used to them at all."—J. M. SYNGE, *The Shadow of the Glen.*

Events are few in the Glen and a valuation is an event. Quite a crowd turned up. Several men shook my hand, wishing me a good valuation, and wished John MacA. the same—which seemed to be asking much of Providence. John, the outgoing tenant, had lived in the Argentine and spoke three languages. It was the west coast climate as much as anything that was driving him east. The unofficial president to whom everyone turned was Tom MacB., shepherd at Fernaig (the farm down the Glen). I had not previously met him, but had heard him. Indeed, one would have to be very deaf to enter this part of Lochalsh without hearing Tom when he was working his dogs wide out. His friends said that once when he had really shouted the Navy had manned the guns at Kyle ; and seemingly his voice at seventy was a mere echo of its former self. Despite his years he was working the sheep on a hill beside which Achbeg was a back garden. I never heard his opinions on sheep matters mentioned without the deepest respect. At a valuation, of course, whisky is passed around and Donald had warned me that Tom was a terrible man without his dram. All my cycling and phoning produced nothing better than a few bottles of a far milder fluid, but they served. The shepherd was as quiet as a lamb, and I should have known that my leg was being pulled.

There were crops, dung and oddments to be valued, but by far the chief item was the sheep flock, of which more in a moment. It is common for each party to appoint a valuator, a thirdsman being called in in case of disagreement, but John and I had adopted the cheaper course of binding ourselves to accept the ruling of one professional valuator. No ewes having been cast the previous autumn the valuator handled every ewe to make sure she was " sound in the mouth and sound below." I had arranged for a man to mark the lambs while they were ready.

John departed, we moved in, and a lull followed. It was too early for the hay, and on " the hill " there was little to do but take an occasional look at the sheep. We spent the time settling in, preparing apparatus for hay-making, and learning something about the job we had undertaken.

There may be readers who know as little about the general pattern of hill-sheep farming as we did to begin with. A brief account of it may be of use to them ; others will skip the next few paragraphs.

First, as I have said, our sheep were hill Cheviots, which have a soft, long-staple wool like that of Lowland Cheviots, but are almost as hardy as the Blackface breed. (Lowland sheep, if transferred to the poor grazing of the hills, would at once melt away.) Some districts have Black-face, some have Cheviot, and some are mixed. The relative merits of the two breeds are much discussed by sheep men.

Second, our flock was tied to the ground ; it must be taken over from an outgoing tenant by his successor, or failing a successor by the landlord, the price to include acclimatization value. This last is a considerable factor, as sheep are worth more on their own ground than in the ring—in extreme cases, even double. If the Achbeg flock were interchanged with a similar flock in another county, both flocks would suffer. To begin with they would take every chance of straying, usually homewards. They might die of infections to which they had not acquired immunity. They would not know where to go for early grass, late grass, or rough feed breaking the snow, and they would not know the best stream crossings. Ewes at the best are strangely stupid about leading new-born lambs over a flood they themselves can hardly ford, but at least when on their own ground they are guided by habit to the easiest places. For these and other reasons acclimatization is highly important.

Third, our flock, being tied to the ground, was necessarily a breeding stock and not a flying stock. A farmer may buy in ewes from outside, take one or two lambs and fleeces from each, and sell them again, lambs and all; there is thus no continuity in a flying stock. A breeding stock maintains itself indefinitely. What happens may be illustrated most simply by following briefly the history of an individual ewe lamb.

Her life is dominated by the seasonal rhythm of too much and too little. She will have been born in late April or in May : not later, because she would miss some of the benefit of the summer flush of grazing—not sooner, because her mother cannot be asked to feed two mouths on bog-cotton and heather-shoots. Shepherds watch the hill grass very closely in April. The lambs will come as surely as the tortoise, but the weather (and consequently the grass) is more erratic than any hare. A late season, or worse still a false start, may kill many lambs.

After a few days the lamb begins to nibble at grass, but her mother continues to bear the chief strain of feeding her throughout the summer. She will be taken off her mother in August in order that the ewe may build up strength for the winter. This first winter is the most critical time in the life of the lamb, or rather the hogg, as she now begins to be called. If she is poorly fed, and especially if she is left to pick up what she can on the hill, she will be stunted in her growth : a poor milker throughout life and poor mutton after. There are also deficiency diseases that are dangerous to hoggs on the west. Accordingly she goes off (like the swallows and the shooting tenants) to a kindlier district for the winter, usually to the Black Isle or similar arable country. There she will be in clover in every sense until Christmas, after which she will be folded on roots and kale. Poor ground indeed her native hill must seem when she returns in early April. She will remember the ground, but will not join up with her mother again. Farmers who for one reason or another winter their hoggs at home, none the less separate them from their mothers for a week or two until the milk flow of the ewes has ceased; the hoggs and their mothers pair off again in an affection that can now only be called Platonic.

As a hogg she will have a thick fleece that must be shorn early for her comfort and safety. By autumn, when she begins to be called a gimmer, she will be approaching her full size. However, the second winter is only less critical than the first. By unlucky chance sheep are expected to carry lambs just when feed is at its poorest : the ewe about to lamb after a bad winter on bad ground, may actually weigh less than in the autumn, which must mean that she has created the lamb out of her own substance. The strain would be too much for the average gimmer. In most flocks only a few of the best gimmers are allowed to be on the hill in November and December, when the tups are out with the ewes, and the others lead a more cloistered life in parks with good high walls until the tups are brought in again.

Next summer she becomes a " second gimmer " and is at the top of her form if she has not been allowed to lamb. She will be left on the hill during the tupping season of her third winter, and will thus produce her first lamb when she is just three years old. In the autumn her lamb will be taken from her, she will be desolated for a few days, and will then pick up condition and caper around as in earlier times. But the winter will find her with a much poorer reserve than she had twelve months previously. She may be so weak by spring that a man may easily catch her in open country without a dog. She may have difficulty in getting up if she has lain in a hollow. Her second lamb will be born when she is just four years old ; she will feed it through the summer, undergo the same deprivation and holiday, and enter her fifth winter somewhat past her prime. At five years old she will bear her third lamb and at six her fourth—unless she fails to conceive and is " eild " in any particular year, and unless she varies the routine by having twins.

She is becoming rather old for the hard conditions of hill life. She may be given one more year if she is in relatively good strip and her teeth are still sound, but she will more likely be sold as a cast ewe. She will probably be bought by a low-ground farmer who will keep her in parks, feed her well, and take one or two more lambs off her, possibly by a heavier tup such as a Border Leicester ; or she may be fattened and " graded " (sold for slaughter) immediately ; or she may even be graded direct from the hill if her condition permits. If, however, the flock is not very well managed she may be left for several years more on the hill, to become a flop-eared, scraggy and supremely canny matriarch. There was a twelve-year-old Blackface that haunted a farm we knew, mere bones and wool and black looks, and said to be a witch. She eventually perished in the snow.

Such is the history of a typical ewe, bearing four lambs and being cast at six-and-a-half. Not all of the ewe lambs born in a given year, however, are needed to maintain the flock. The surplus, perhaps a third, will be sold in their first autumn, possibly to hill farmers setting up a stock, more probably to low-ground farmers who will breed from them cross lambs such as the famous Scotch Half Bred (Border Leicester cross). A considerable part of the sheep population of low farms is drawn in this way from the hardy hill stocks.

The fate of the male or tup lambs is quite different. At the end of May they are castrated and so become wedders. In their first autumn, nowadays, wedders are usually sold, fattened and graded. The modern small family requires a small joint, unluckily for the wedder lamb. A few will be kept back from sale and allowed to reach the age of two or three. Health regulations permit only a licenced butcher to kill sheep, and during the war farmers were forbidden to do so for the added reason that a good wedder represented anything up to a two-year

meat ration. However, wedders would at certain times
of the year, such as potato lifting, leap from rocks, run
under cars, or die suddenly of braxy. Two crofters on
the Island were heavily fined for killing a sheep. We were
able to observe, however, that the mortality was uniform
in the sheep of those who make the law, those who ad-
minister it, and those upon whom it is administered. The
two crofters were merely hastening a course that Nature
would have taken in any case.

Finally there are the tups, or rams, the only sheep not
bred on the farm. They are, of course, the key to the
flock, and are chosen with great care. They are fed well
in the autumn and put out to the hill in November and
December. After two seasons they are shifted or sold,
to prevent their breeding with their own progeny.

The shepherd thinks of sheep, but the farmer thinks
at least as much of money. A breeding flock brings in
four cheques a year—on the wool, the lambs, the cast
ewes and the hill sheep subsidy. By chance the four cheques
were about equal in our first year. The chief expense other
than rent, is the wintering of the hoggs, which rose to
almost £1 per head (including freight) while we were at
Achbeg. There is also the rapid drop in value of the tups,
and on a large farm there would be wages and dip. A
small farmer often arranges to come in at the tail end of
a bigger dipping in return for his labour at the dipping,
and pays no wages.

Any shepherd knows every one of his ewes and her
parentage and history. " Do you remember the tup from
Roddy MacB.'s that got in the bog ? This was the best
lamb he ever left," pointing maybe to a mature beldam.
" It was her mother that lost both ears to the fox." So
I spent part of the lull looking at our sheep and wondering
if I should ever know one from another. A few were
unmistakable. One had a belly as bare as a pig's, and
another had lost all her wool except for a tuft on the tail.
Several had lost the wool at the neck so that their heads
poked nakedly forward like that of a tortoise. There were

also two Blackface crosses, one of them a creature of great character who came to be called Blackie. Only gradually did the flock take shape. There are no wrinkles on an old ewe to mark her off from the hoggs and gimmers, but age somehow stamps itself on anything. There were differences of wool, size and bearing, but I never reached the stage of knowing them by their expressions. Any keen boy brought up on a sheep farm knows more at the age of ten.

My helper on the hill at first was Major, a large collie left behind by John. Major had winning habits, in particular a trick of going through the motion of barking without making a sound, but he was a " coarse " sheep-dog, hard on the sheep and unbiddable. Donald taught me the calls and gestures for working him. I well recall my surprise to find that Major took me for a shepherd. I shouted and pointed—and off he went. It was almost disconcerting. But he was self-willed, and preferred to do the organising himself. Though he never bit a sheep, he did the next worst thing. A single ewe, like a single human, is far less manageable than a group. When one bolted off alone Major followed at all costs. Once he chased a ewe that had bolted down past the Falls out of sight. I found the dog, but not the sheep. A week or two later a carcase began to advertise itself at a floodgate downstream.

There was also the hill to explore. It was necessary to learn at first to identify on the site particular spots seen from the house. A cairn marked Craig Mheol (pronounced roughly Crick Vowel), the summit, about 800 feet up. It gave a fine panorama of sea, islands and cliffs, with the Applecross hills and the Coolins dwarfing all else. In some lights the Coolins suggested great icebergs sailing by, an illusion that only heightened the sense of their tremendous bulk.

We found a methylated spirit bottle at Creag Mheol at about Christmas. The grass under it was still fresh. Had some connoisseur of views, with an inner warmth to hold back the outer cold, conducted a Christmas orgy there ?

An old peat-hag with wretched bent-grass that the sheep rarely touched extended for perhaps fifty fairly level acres on top of the hill, and its old workings made the going rather treacherous after dark. It ended in the scarp that faced the house on the south; cliffs and rocks with good grass on one-time scree. There were many sheltered hollows here where it was easy to overlook a sheep. On the east slope much better grass ran down to the Strome-ferry road, as the tilt of the strata gave an unbroken surface here. On the west a green saddle linked our hill to the cone of the Portachullin hill, the common grazing of the Portachullin crofters. On the fourth side, the north, was Strome Wood, covering a scarp that corresponded roughly to the cliffs facing the house. The remains of a burnt-out fence marked the edge of the wood; any sheep at all could jump it, and I was soon to learn a good deal about Strome Wood.

Between the Face, or scarp, and the house lay the Flat, some 30 acres of rough grazing, doubtless the top of the great block that had sunk a thousand feet when a fault created the Glen. From the cliffs it was easy to pick out traces of buildings, enclosures, tracks, lazy-beds and other cultivation marks, but now there was nothing but patchy grazing.

All in all it was a poor-to-medium hill, quite adequately stocked at a sheep to two acres. It was inclined to dry out, had too much bracken, bent and rashes, and even the cotton-grass on the bogs, which is supposed to give the first spring bite, the sheep rarely tasted—why, I do not know. It had little shelter on windy days. But at least it was a clean hill, free from disease. The chief thing it taught me was the pleasure of looking at a really good sheep hill.

Park sheep can be handled at any time, but with hill sheep the gathering may be the main part of the work. Accordingly advantage is taken of a valuation gathering to get the lambs marked. Each of our ewe lambs had a small piece taken out of the top of the left ear, a " left tip " having been chosen as our flock-mark. The tup lambs, who would soon be leaving the flock, were given a different mark. They were also castrated by the teeth-and-penknife method. Some sheep men prefer bloodless castration with a special instrument, but it is not wholly reliable. No anaesthetics are used. By either method it is an unedifying business, but farming would be chaos without it. Provided a good day is chosen, dry but not too hot, the lambs recover rapidly, and losses are rare. All tails were docked for cleanliness, with a kitchen knife. The tails of ewe and wedder lambs thrown into separate buckets provided a tally. Finally, all the ewes were given the new flock-mark. A gathering of hill sheep may or may not leave a few behind on ledges or among trees, and it is understood that any later found unmarked will be paid for by the new tenant. Altogether the marking is a thorough-going spring rite, the goriness being gratuitously added to by red keel. Though the earmark is always the final test, a second mark more readily picked out from a distance is needed. Every sheep was given a dab of keel (special colouring matter) on the " right rib." Donald's keel-mark was on the left rib and his earmark a right tip. Thus we had no difficulty in distinguishing our sheep when they mixed, as they always did.

The hoggs, with their healthy pride of bearing, were a pleasure even to my unpractised eye. No expensive lady ever wore a magnificent coat with more assurance. But the coat becomes a danger to them when the heat brings forth the flies, and the first sheep work of the summer is therefore the hogg-clipping. Just as soon as the new growth, known as the rise, makes shearing possible, the work begins.

I went to help Tom at " the white house," the shell of a cottage converted to a clipping shed. The hoggs were penned on one side and on the other was a row of about five low clipping-stools. Tom had pride of place at the unglazed window, from which he had a view of Applecross, Fernaig and the road. Several neighbours who had come to help sat on the other stools. To me and another man fell the humble job of crogging, that is, keeping the clippers supplied with sheep. The occasion is a blend of barbering and all-in wrestling. There is knack in catching sheep and carrying them, but they seem to be twice the weight towards evening. Luckily there is plenty of time for a breather between one burden and the next. Conversation was in Gaelic or in English, according to the need of the moment.

For me the work had the added interest of novelty, but I still enjoy the unsteady snip-snip, the muttered conversation, the oily smell of the sheep, and the slow thinning of the numbers in the pen. Most of all I like to watch the transformation on the clipping-stool. Three legs are tied ; the brownish fleece is peeled from the belly backwards, the hogg is swung over to her other side, and there she lies, egg-shaped and dazzlingly white on the curdled fleece, like a spirit freed from its clay.

" Buist ! " calls the shearer as he finishes. A black symbol, the buist, is stamped on her flank or rib or shoulder, any cuts are dressed with Stockholm tar to repel flies, and she makes uncertainly for her shorn peers. The fleece is rolled, thrown on a pile, and later bagged. I sometimes took a turn at bagging. A wool-bag over six feet long is slung from the rafters. A man drops inside, stamps down the fleeces passed to him and slowly works out of his cocoon.

We were at the Fernaig hoggs for part of two more days, and then came the turn of the Achbeg hoggs. Donald's flock, being a flying stock, had no hoggs.

Early on a perfect June morning, four of us set out to gather—Donald, Tom, a crofter named Duncan, and myself. Four men for a hundred sheep on two hundred acres. But ten men could not have made sure of a 100 per cent. gathering. It was not the hill itself that created the difficulty ; indeed, I sometimes gathered the hill alone later on when I had a good dog. It was Strome Wood that created the difficulty. The march fence had been

Crofter's horse. Prince always expected his "piece" at the kitchen door.

Heather-burning. Snow still lies on the hills around Ree Breac.

Ploughing rough lea. A government subsidy encouraged the ploughing of old leas.

Prima. The first calf born on our farm, now nearing her own first calving.

burned in a forest fire, and I imagine there had been loose wires before that. (Where there is parched hill ground on one side of a fence and brilliant green grass on the other, staples have a way of falling out.) The luscious blades, bunched tight and fully eight inches high in the clearings, were a revelation to me. Our sheep were more in the wood than on the hill.

We started by clearing another park above Stromeferry where our sheep wandered freely, oblivious of the niceties of rent and ownership, and also the odd corners in Stromeferry itself. The ungated road allowed them down to the shore there, and often they grazed railway verges and even private gardens. Myriads of dew-drops on the birch-twigs were flashing prismatic colours and the morning haze still softened the granite outlines of Gladstone's Face, the mountain-side across the loch. We soon had the sheep out of the smaller enclosure but Strome Wood was another story. It has cliffs, scree, dense plantations, fallen trees, patches of bog, and every natural object likely to give sheep the laugh over men. The whole wood is set at a steep angle, shooting from our march fence at 800 feet down to the railway at the shore's edge. Duncan came through the wood from its Portachullin end and the other three of us worked along in a diagonal formation from the Strome end. Donald on the fire-track at the bottom made loud noises to put my sheep up-hill. I followed at the mid level, somewhat behind, and did the same; while Tom took the cart-track near the top to deal with the sheep as they came out there. Our general plan was to drive them to the large burnt-out clearing known as the Mill, where they would easily be forced out at the top on to Achbeg. The sheep knew what was afoot, and they knew that a gathering usually means something unpleasant. Many of them doubled back along familiar hidden sheep-walks; there was a great deal of hulloing, barking, and beating around before we were satisfied that all or nearly all were out. The rest of the gathering was easy, though the ledges of the Face often call for further skilled work with the

C

dogs. The many bunches of sheep and lambs were merged into one mass and brought down the funnel-hollow to the road at the Well. Ewes and their lambs were always getting separated in the crush. Within the overall movement of the flock there was an endless churning as bleating ewe sought piping lamb, and, having found it, lost it again.

At the steading we drew out the hoggs and eild ewes and put the others back to the hill. The rise naturally comes later on a ewe feeding a lamb. The clipping was done beside the gable of the steading, under the blue sky but out of the glare of the sun. I rolled the fleeces on a tarpaulin. Each is rolled in a particular way, and a tail is twisted out of the fleece to bind it into a compact parcel. A gratifying mound of fleeces had grown by evening, the more gratifying because there would be no bother in selling it : the Wool Control bought the country's whole clip at standard prices. An argument developed, I remember, about a particular ewe : one neighbour maintained that she had been a certain pet lamb, and another that there was no resemblance. And Tom was envied for his idyllic life :

> " Lazy shepherd of the hill,
> That never worked and never will,"

as the rhyme unjustly runs.

A few weeks later the remaining ewes of the various flocks in the Glen were shorn, Donald's and ours being gathered and clipped in a single day. His sheep ground was not a hill but an extensive bog by the river, and his gathering was straightforward enough. In the meantime clipping had been made urgent by the onset of maggot. Perhaps I have given the impression already that sheep work is a job for Dresden shepherdesses. If so, it is time for me to say something of maggot, first advising those to whom vicarious pain is unendurable to omit a page or two.

My only earlier experience of maggot had been the sight of a dying Blackface on the Island. In the side of her belly was a raw pit in which seethed a filthy yellowish mass of maggots. They swarmed in the centre, each wriggling over others and being engulfed by yet more ; and those at the edges crawled not only between and through the muscles but actually into the vital organs. Many had their heads down and were feeding on the living flesh. The ewe had sunk into a stupor, and her bewildered lamb was nuzzling its coal-black face into the empty udder. I have seen plenty of cases of maggot since, a few of them worse, and I consider it the one wholly revolting thing in farm work. To anyone who believes that all's right with the world I recommend a summer holiday with hill sheep.

It has only recently become a serious problem. Certain species of green-bottle and blue-bottle have taken to laying their eggs in the wool of sheep. Any smell, due for instance to dirty wool round the tail, adds to the danger. In a day or two the eggs hatch into maggots the size of a printed comma. They rapidly grow to a quarter or half an inch in length. Fear and irritation cause the ewe to sweat, and more flies are attracted. Clusters of crisp yellow globes of eggs appear around the original strike. If the trouble is not found in time there will be thousands—from the look of them one might say millions—of maggots in the wool. For a while they seem to live on the moisture of the wool but they soon form into clusters with their heads down into the flesh and their tails out. Pocks, rapidly growing in size and number, are made in a widening area of skin. The attack once begun, more and more flies add their eggs. There is no mercy, and no relief but death or the shepherd's aid. Buzzards take over from the maggots, and within a week or two a lovely hogg has become nothing but a white stain in the heather. Buzzards are magnificent birds, but their screeching and wheeling so often drew my attention to a sheep lost in the bracken that I became conditioned to hate them as keenly as a keeper.

It is just the healthiest animals, the hoggs and gimmers with their glossy wool, that most attract the flies. An occasional sheep may scrape herself free of the maggots at the beginning of a strike, but she will worry herself thin in the attempt, and very few succeed. There is nothing for it but preventive dipping, vigilance throughout the bad season, and prompt treatment. Losses have been growing so heavy of late years that the words of an old Highland seer may yet prove true. He said that a day would come when men in the Highlands would not know the look of a sheep (though it is quite as likely that the sheep will forget the look of a man).

Vigilance is not easy. Even with park sheep, I believe, endless care is needed to keep a flock clean. In hill conditions, complete certainty is almost impossible for a shepherd, and quite impossible for a crofter. With all the summer work in the fields to attend to he cannot be searching every hollow, every patch of bracken and scrub, day in and day out. At one stage the ewe likes a knoll, where the breeze can cool her sweating skin, but mostly she buries herself deep in bracken or similar cover. She often ignores the dog, and hours of beating around may fail to dislodge her. Sometimes the first clue is an ear poking out of the bracken ; and sometimes what first comes out of the bracken is the smell of ammonia. Many times I heard of dead sheep later found within a few yards of where searchers had passed. It would be worth while training pointers or spaniels to locate sheep on such occasions, but I never heard of dogs so employed, except in snowdrifts.

It was Donald, as usual, who taught me the symptoms. A stricken ewe changes her bearing like any other sick animal. The curves of health give way to the angularity of sickness, and her head is no longer carried high. She is much alone, and often runs long distances for no obvious reason. There is one almost infallible symptom, a certain toss of the head. Either grazing or lying undisturbed, she turns her head quickly towards her shoulder, but instead of nibbling after a tick she inhibits the movement halfway. Just occasionally great heat leads to similar behaviour, but nearly always it is the mark of trouble. Once the sheep have been disturbed their behaviour becomes untypical, and I found that a pair of binoculars repaid their cost in a month. A ewe noticed on a spur of rock may need immediate attention, but if she is quietly chewing the cud, all is well.

Once identified the stricken sheep are brought in with a bunch of others to a pen. Ideally the maggots should be scraped out of the fleece into running water, where the fish will eat them, but with half a dozen to be seen to just when the hay is running to stem and seed, that method would be too slow. Instead, special dip is poured on to the affected part, to drive out the maggots. Many people prefer a dearer balsam, both because it promotes healing and because it leaves fewer dead maggots to decompose in the fleece and attract more flies. Great care must be taken to find every small pocket of maggots ; even one overlooked would be the start of further strikes. The fleece is therefore parted flock by flock, in suspected quarters ; and by pressing an ear to the fleece you can often pick out a quiet hissing against the thumps of the heart. All eggs must be pinched, and the treated ewes are best kept in a park where they can be observed for a while. They are a special target. If the area of skin damaged has become too great, nothing can save the ewe and she is best destroyed forthwith ; but we witnessed some remarkable recoveries. Donald had a tup who was very badly affected, but he refused to die and, in the teeth of all probability, lived to be father of many fine lambs.

The trouble began gradually. First there were one or two false alarms ; then I found a ewe hiding under brambles, too far gone to be saved. We were dressing her long after midnight, in the faint light from the north, but she died before morning. Several others followed, both ours and Donald's. We cleaned them up, watched them, cleaned them up again, and at length turned them loose, with bare patches of size varying from a few square inches to that of a dinner-plate. Next there was a dead ewe high on one of the ledges. Before I could bury her the buzzards, or more likely a wild-cat or a fox, had removed the head and neck complete. I found the grisly object at a neighbour's garden gate a few days later.

Our hill and Donald's bog were moderately easy to patrol, but I now began to pay heavily for the free grazing in Strome Wood. Besides all the former obstacles there were now acres and acres of bracken waist high and soon shoulder high. There could be no question of seeing every ewe in the wood. In the autumn, when the bracken had died down, I found the remains of several. One had caught a hind leg in the cleft of a fallen tree and had died half-hanging down the hill. Her fate was probably the least unpleasant. When we saw a stricken sheep we might be lucky and get her out at the Mill; more often she kept us chasing back and forth for half a day and more. We eventually cornered one ewe on a ledge of a cliff, but she defeated us by leaping to her death. July and August went by. Strikes were becoming so frequent that we abandoned nearly all other work to see to the sheep. In sun and rain, wind and calm, we plunged around in the wood until at length the turning point came. By September we could relax. It had been the worst year for maggot ever known. That it should have been my first year with sheep was one of our few pieces of really bad luck. We decided to ask the Forestry men to repair the fence before summer.

To return to the clipping, then, we decided to get it done as early as possible. Sultry weather is the worst for maggot, and the winter fleece, besides causing the ewe to sweat, gives the eggs a better milieu. Once shorn the ewe is fairly safe for a week or two, though we did occasionally find casualties within two days of clipping.

The ewes had not such good fleeces as the hoggs. Indeed, some had none at all, having left them in small tatters through Strome Wood where they gave pleasure to none but nesting birds. Ours were not the barest sheep I have seen, however. I remember looking at a bunch of fifteen or twenty that had just come out of a young larch plantation. Some had poodle tufts; some a few flocks here and there on the flanks or rump. I doubt whether they had the equivalent of a fleece among them, and I am certain they had not the components of a whole fleece. Such animals add little to the wool-cheque, though they do well enough on the other three scores.

The other precaution that can be taken is dipping. There are two compulsory dippings, one in the summer and one in winter, at which a policeman should be present; but the police could not possibly attend every dipping in the huge area under their supervision; still less could they certify that every gathering had brought in every sheep. The chief purpose of the compulsory dip is to prevent scabies. Any scab-mites on the sheep are killed by the dip, and a second dipping ten days later would kill any mites that had hatched out from eggs in the wool, before they in turn could lay eggs. By one of those astonishing compromises of the British, only one dipping is compulsory, the other being demanded if scab has been reported in the district but not otherwise. The dip also kills ticks, maggots (not eggs, unfortunately) and the other parasites that are omitted from pastoral poetry. In bad maggot seasons, farmers often arrange an extra dipping, since the smell of the dip keeps off flies for a week or two—if they are lucky. The actual immersion in anything so unpleasant can hardly be good for the sheep, but the freedom from parasites often causes them to pick up condition almost from the day of dipping.

Dip is expensive. Quite apart from the dip that remains in the fleeces there is a considerable quantity left over in the dipping-bath that is useless except for any " white " ewes missed at the gathering and picked up later. Hence we arranged to join in with neighbours, usually Fernaig, occasionally Braientra.

Visitors to hill sheep country must often have been puzzled by the fanks. They look like the beginning of a huge and massive house abandoned at shoulder height, except that they follow the tilt of ground. The rooms are a system of pens, large and small. In the centre there is a broad corridor in which batches of sheep can conveniently be handled and there is usually an ingenious device called a shedder. A partition leaves a channel in which sheep can travel in single file only. They are urged on from behind, while a shepherd swings a gate to and fro. It makes possible very rapid sorting—say lambs in one pen, ewes in another; " stragglers " can be picked out from the flock, or two hirsels (working units) separated. Highland fanks are simple, and usually rather dilapidated. Wear and tear are heavy; gates are soon broken by over-lively sheep and stack-rope and stones do the work of hinges and hasps, but the work gets done all the same. Probably no part of the farm is so heavily dunged as the fank. It has usually emerald grass, or a phalanx of thistles (for Nature does not discriminate against weeds), and rain carries the influence of the dung in a meandering green streak down the hill.

Donald helped to gather our neighbours' sheep ; but without knowing the ground I should have been worse than useless on the thousands of rolling acres up in the hills. The sheep were first forced into the largest pen ; then with much hulloing and barking, " cuts " would be driven through the shedder to smaller pens. From there they would pass in small batches to the dipping pen itself. The younger sheep travelled fairly readily, but the older sheep knew the moves all too well. They hung back as successive cuts went through until the residue was largely " pops "—old sheep bearing the small dot that marks the cast ewe. What a time they gave us ! On over a dozen occasions before they had been through it all. They had learned, not only the horrors of the bath, but a hundred tricks for foiling humans. They would run anywhere but towards the smell of the dip. " Now, close in, lads ! Hey up, ewies—hi, she's away— that's the lot of them. We'll try again . . . " Finally we might have to catch them one by one and carry them through by main force. There was always one final hope for the ewe; she might leap clean over the bath to momentary freedom. At once almost the whole lot of us, and as many dogs as men, would try to corner her, or to drive her to a small batch let loose for the purpose. But she usually knew all about that too, and led us a merry chase before we caught her. There is more work in dipping twenty old " pops " than fifty lively hoggs.

Tom, in a waterproof yellow cassock, superintended the actual immersion. He seemed to have a feeling of responsibility for all the sheep, his own and others', and was never at ease till the whole of the dipping or clipping in the Strath was done. He stood at a lower level on one side of the bath while the croggers passed the sheep down to him, one by one. The ewe was let down into the opaque grey-brown liquid, back first, staring skywards in her terror. A half-somersault brought her right-side-up, while Tom kept a hand on her face to make certain it went under in the turn. The ewe floundered along for a couple of yards and dragged her unwonted weight up the slope to the dripping-pen. Here she stood for a few minutes with a crowd of others, until most of the surplus dip had drained back into the bath. Meanwhile the second dripping-pen would be filling with another batch. Every now and then a sheep would kick at the wrong moment, just as she touched the surface of the dip, and a spout would shoot up into Tom's face. He never grumbled. He would slide his cap forward, wipe his eyes with the back of it, replace it on his forehead, spit out any dip that had got into his mouth, and take the next sheep. The other men would pretend to think the crogger had been working out a grudge against him. Often enough I saw a foot slip or stumble at the edge of the bath, but I never saw a man fall in; I fancy he would blink and leap in the dipping-pen as the sheep do when the dip is too strong. That is the rather rough-and-ready test often applied for the strength of the bath!

Crogging at the fank is heavy work. At the beginning of each penful, the sheep are close-packed and easily caught. They get more freedom of movement as they thin out, and do everything they can to be difficult. Tom's ewes were heavier than ours, his ground being far better, and the tups were about all a man can lift. How the dipping is done with the heavy breeds of lowland sheep I cannot imagine, unless there are devices to obviate the lifting. When there were enough men at the fank we took turns at the crogging, and argument and banter kept the day from seeming too long.

Our own sheep went through last. The dip kept its potency against scab and ticks to the end, but I was never so sure about its value for repelling the fly. " The first cut of the cake is the best," as I heard a shepherd put it. By evening of the second day the bath is none too savoury. There must have been a balance of gain, however, since strikes were infrequent for a while afterwards.

Marking, clipping, dipping and the war against maggot make up the bulk of the summer sheep work. Some days will begin with a gathering in the early morning, and end with a search for a ewe long after sunset. One evening we finished gathering the Achbeg sheep in virtual darkness, often stumbling into the peat-workings in the effort to intercept phantom sheep. We were guided by the bleating and barking more than by sight. At other times the sheep would require little attention for many days on end, until the maggot scare began. At length came a gathering for quite another purpose ; but that leads us to the important question of sales, which must wait till a later chapter.

CHAPTER IV

CATTLE

> " And, behold, there came out of the river seven kine, fatfleshed
> and well favoured ; and they fed in a meadow ; and, behold, seven
> other kine came up after them, poor and very ill-favoured and
> leanfleshed, such as I never saw in the land of Egypt for badness."
> " Genesis."

We sold milk ; but that isn't as obvious as it sounds.
In earlier days, when money entered little into the life
of the place, and when practically every family had its
croft, it was the custom in the Highlands for any house-
holder who had milk, to give it to those whose cows were
dry ; and any suggestion of payment would have been
rightly resented. Conditions have changed now. In our
district there were railway workers, Forestry workers and
various others who had no croft, and on the other hand,
purchased goods have gained greatly in importance on
crofts also. To adhere strictly to the tradition of mutual
help in kind would no longer be practicable, and indeed
milk was brought by train across the breadth of Scotland.
Though the railway workers were allowed free transport,
some people were paying 1s. 1d. for a pint—4d. for the
milk and 9d. for freight ! However, the feeling against
milk-sales survives and we should have had too much
respect for its origin to take any initiative (in-comers as
we were) in breaking it down.

It chanced that there was no need, because we inherited
from John a retail milk connection that made a great difference to Achbeg—almost the difference between profit and
loss. We charged a steady 4d. a pint summer and winter.
Thus a cow who enabled us to sell even 12 pints a day
brought us in perhaps £30 or £40 during the summer.
The alternative use for the milk would have been to feed
a calf, and no calf of ours ever put half that sum of money

on to its ribs in a summer. Takings of course are not all profit, in the one case or the other; but we had no delivery costs as our customers called for the milk, and there was no deduction for freight or commission. Apart from extra work (and on a croft time and money are not freely interchangeable) our only considerable added cost was the more extravagant use of winter feeding. Of this more must be said shortly.

Knowing the value of direct milk sales, and supposing —quite wrongly—that we might lose all our customers if there were any break in the supply at our taking over, we were anxious to have one or two cows in milk from the very outset. Naturally we had a preference for good milkers, but at a pinch any cow was likely to be better than none : the purchase cost of an average cow may be covered by the extra milk sales she makes possible in a matter of a few months and is thus no very great matter.

Cows were hard to come by. With the grass and the subsidy both coming on, nobody was in a hurry to sell. There were other difficulties too. When a cow is sold at any time, the owner usually has a good reason for parting with her, and caution was needed. Moreover we could not go far afield in our search. Cows accustomed to better weather, better grazing, and a higher standard of living generally are apt to " melt away " when brought into the harder conditions of Wester Ross, even if they do not take red-water fever. There are ticks in the area that carry the infection. Cows born within the area, or brought in as calves, acquire a fair immunity, but full-grown cows brought in may take ill and die at once. Hence our choice was limited, and we followed up every rumour of a cow for sale.

Cheetah was our first purchase. I cycled over to a croft by Loch Alsh to inspect her. She was a black poll (poll Angus, or Aberdeen Angus), with little or no admixture of other blood, and that she was no breaker of yield records was plain to my unprofessional eye : she had a dainty, built-in udder like that of a mare (I never can under-

stand how a mare builds up a strapping quarter-ton foal
with so little outward show of means), and the general
build of a Department bull fresh from wintering. She was,
in fact, what Donald later dubbed her, a great bag of beef,
and as such I bought her. She had recently calved and
was giving a gallon-and-a-half a day. Thus she would help
us to tide over the first shortage and at worst we could
grade her for beef. Poor Cheetah! She was a charming,
skittish companion with endearing ways, and in particular
a habit of roaring innocent challenges to all strange cows
within sight. But she was emphatically no milker. After
the first flush during which her yield soared to two gallons
for a few days, she always settled down for the rest of her
lactation as the general provider of the byre-cats. In the
end we did grade her (that is, sell her by weight to the
Ministry of Food), and such was her bulk that we were
only ten shillings down on her purchase price.

Maundy, on the other hand, had the lines of a real
milker. She was a half-Guernsey poll, due to produce
her second calf in a month or so, and as beautiful as any
creature in her prime and in tip-top condition. Her former
owner kept few beasts and treated them well. There was
also Ruby, an elderly Shorthorn, a good milker who
mothered the two youngsters. When something in the
morning air set them kicking up the turf and scampering
over the banks, Ruby maintained the dignity proper to
her age. To these three initial purchases were added
others later, and there were, of course, the calves and
stirks that were born on the farm, but they remained the
nucleus of the stock throughout.

To a farmer a cow is first and foremost a business
proposition, but she is also a personality—Cheetah,
Maundy, or Ruby, skittish, sentimental or staid. One
thing all cows have in common is a ruthless propensity
to bully. Like most townsmen I used to fancy that the
cow was the most placid of all creatures, and so at times
it is. There is something soothing about milking at any
season ; and in winter the byre had the exaggerated calm

of a chapel. Outside was the commotion of the elements, all blackness and threatened disaster; inside, the orderly row of buttocks in the upward light of the lantern, the gently rocking shadows, the measured scrunching of hay, first gobbled down and now enjoyed at leisure, and the soft purring of the milk in the pail. Alien sounds—the chink of a tossed chain, and the intermittent rumbles in the pressed bellies—stand out as highlights, separate yet belonging.

But it is a precarious calm. Let Ruby's chain come undone and little unoffending Prima in the twin-stall will be gored till her roars pass into screaming. I have rarely heard sounds more full of terror than those from a chained beast beside an unchained superior. For it is all a question of social standing. I forget who wrote:

> " I love the cow and her relations;
> They chew the cud and know their stations,"

but he was no farmer. At first glance you might imagine that a herd of cows on a road was thinking only of clover and eternity, but watch them when they reach a gate and you will learn otherwise. The cows in a herd are spaced out in a social hierarchy or ladder, each claiming, and if necessary exercising, the right to bully every cow below her in status. She behaves worst to the one immediately below her, and is worst treated by that immediately above, for the cows several rungs down present no threat and those several rungs up are beyond immediate ambition. Every cow is merely waiting its chance to move up one, whenever it can muster courage for the challenge, and is determined to take no nonsense from the rung below. At gateways, therefore, an elaborate ritual of " No, after you, dear" is performed, no cow daring to pass immediately in front of a superior. Cattle fight by trying to disembowel one another; hence the niceties of precedence at the gateway, where a presuming cow would present a perfect target. It is said that hand-shaking in humans goes back to the need for immobilising the dagger-hand; possibly all the fuss at doorways has also a utilitarian source. But the equilibrium in the herd is constantly changing, and we had for a while the curious situation in which Ruby bullied Cheetah, Cheetah Maundy and Maundy Ruby, much as the legs in the Isle of Man symbol gyrate eternally in a hopeless mutual pursuit. There is a practical value in watching these social shifts. If on a fenced road you can contrive to arrange the cattle in inverse bullying order, you have only to drive the back animal and the rest need no urging ; whereas you are reduced to hurling stones and threats if the chief bullies are at the front and are disposed to dawdle. We carried a stick the length of a fishing rod but it was not entirely effective, and a peashooter lacks dignity.

Unfortunately I am very bad at haggling ; all I can do is to go through the motions without conviction and therefore without success. There is no virtue in such ineptitude. Every market price rides on a tide of haggling, and it is merely a matter of personal taste whether one prefers to be on deck with the sailors or down with the land-lubbers out of sight of the rude billows. Several years of practice have improved my acting but done little more. Though I no longer spoil a prolonged entertainment by accepting the first figure offered, the final figure always bears an uncomfortable likeness to the first.

We did not own a bull. Our stock of " bovine animals," as a Government regulation calls them, never rose to a dozen, and a bull would not have paid his way. A single bull served the Glen and the neighbouring district, looked after by Donald and lent by the Department of Agriculture for Scotland. At first I did not see the reason for this particular disguised subsidy, the monogamous disposition of humans having diverted my attention from the overwhelming importance of the male in farm stock-breeding.

About 50 or 60 cows would be served each summer by our Township bull ; and a single tup may run with roughly that number of sheep on the hill, and more on enclosed ground. The bull or tup, therefore, contributes roughly the same amount of hereditary equipment to the next generation as 50 cows or ewes and may be reckoned 50 times as important as any one of them : the common saying that the ram is half the flock is true, with the small exception of sex-linked characteristics. The bull is not merely half the herd : if followed through two or three generations, he is all but a quarter or an eighth of the herd—that is to say, he soon *is* the herd so far as heredity goes. A neighbour of ours had bought in some Guernseys a good time before we arrived, but not enough to warrant the keeping of a Guernsey bull. The local black bulls were gradually asserting themselves, and even in our short stay we saw the proportion of black to yellow increasing. Even such purely feminine qualities as milk-capacity in ewes and cows, and egg-laying capacity in hens, can be fostered chiefly through progeny-testing of the male, though naturally culling of the females is also important.

The male breeding animals, then, are the key to live-stock quality. When bulls fetch 14,000 guineas in the ring, the buyer is really paying for the milk that his progeny will produce—or even for the bulls he will father, to be bought in their turn for the milk they will indirectly produce. Except, of course, when he is merely advertising.

Good bulls are bred or bought by the Department of Agriculture and lent to crofting townships. Running expenses (feed, transport and insurance) are met by the crofters' Committee but the depreciation of the bull is borne by the Government. In this way it is hoped in a few cow-generations to raise the quality of the stock more rapidly than could be achieved through commercial bulls (though these, too, must always be licensed now). A cow-generation may be anything from 3 years to over 10, so that in the decade that the scheme has been in operation some calves must have been born that have almost 90 per cent. of " Department blood " in them, while some of the original unaffected cows still live. The form of subsidy is a sound one, in that the increased prosperity arising from the improved stock should eventually mean increased Government revenue. I should add that I had not the

Plockton and Skye. The tree-covered island in the foreground has good coral sand. The Coolins are dimly seen.

Tractor-ploughing. Achbeg house is at the top of the Road Park, and beyond is The Face.

Barn exterior. The Achmore barn had solid walls, large slatted windows, and heather thatch.

Barn interior. Plenty of space for indoor haymaking.

knowledge, nor did I see the cattle for long enough, to judge what improvement is in fact resulting from the scheme.

With hill sheep a generation ranges from 3 to 7 years, and the change in a flock is correspondingly more rapid. If a young man owning a Blackface flock decided to employ only Cheviot tups, he might hope to see practically all noticeable trace of Blackface blood bred out of the flock. Even twenty years later his ewes would be anything from 98 per cent. to 75 per cent. Cheviot. The process of " crossing Blackface out to the Cheviot " is a common method of introducing Cheviots on difficult ground.

We were installed with our three cows, then, and whilst preparing for haymaking we awaited our first important event, the calving of Maundy. We were a little worried to see that her elegance in no way declined as the date drew nearer. Neighbours whom we consulted knew that she *must* be in calf, but were puzzled at her excess of personal discretion.

Then came one of our few pieces of bad luck. The cows had been grazing at Dottacks, the farthest corner of the farm, one hot Sunday early in July. When I fetched them for the evening milking, blood was spurting from one of Maundy's teats. Having chained her in her stall we called in Donald, and started to clean up the wound, a deep transverse cut that continued to bleed freely. No arrangement of ropes would prevent her from kicking wildly whenever we attempted to bathe her. At half-past two next morning, having staunched the wound and strapped it with sticking-plaster, we left the byre for a cup of tea in the kitchen. Donald could have done no more had the cow been his own.

Next morning we 'phoned for the vet, who lived on the other side of Scotland at Dingwall. He was gloomy. The cut had gone through to the milk channel, it was transverse, and the cow was near to calving ; he would put in stitches, but without much hope that they would hold. This time there was no kicking : he stood Donald

D

to keep Maundy's head over her shoulder and me to press on the root of her tail. Unable to arch her spine, she could not begin to kick. I was never more impressed with the value of " knowing how."

Quite how the accident had occurred we did not discover. A ruin containing some sheets of rusty iron stood under the hill at Dottacks. (It had last been inhabited by an old tramp whose name it retained, and one gooseberry bush bore fruit beside it still, sole relic of the former garden.) Perhaps Maundy, maddened by the summer flies, had bundled into the ruin too clumsily in search of shelter. On a large dairy farm such events are no great matter, but they are disasters on a croft. (Everyone was sorry, first for the cow's suffering and second because of the loss to our pocket.)

For some days there was no further incident, and not a sign of the imminence of calving. Then, on the Thursday, young Johnny Ferguson was sent up on his bicycle to tell us of a commotion in the clover field. We hurried over to find Mrs. Ferguson holding off Ruby and Cheetah as best she could. They were anxious to mother a small black calf that was struggling on to wobbly legs in the clover, while Maundy asserted with every promise of aggression that the calf was hers and no other cow's. She was frankly sentimental about it, licked it, stepped aside to defend her rights, and hurried back with a little yearning sound that plainly assured the calf of unbounded, undivided and eternal affection. The affection of animals for their young has for both of us an irresistible appeal. It is one of the greatest joys of farming, and it must be a dull job that entails no comparable pleasure.

But we had, alas, sterner plans for Maundy. As a half-Guernsey, she was meant to be a milker or house-cow, not a sucker—a distinction to which I must return in a moment. In spite of Maundy's ceaseless demonstrations we trundled the calf to the byre, where a pen of clean straw was ready, and chained Maundy in her stall. She was indignant and continued to utter the yearning signals, to which the calf made no response. We gave her a warm drink and left her to settle down. When the time came to draw off some milk—not too much at first for fear of milk fever—she held back, wanting her calf and no bucket ; then changing her mind, she suddenly " let down," and only the one quarter offered any difficulty.

The milk of Guernseys has so much cream in it that an odd Guernsey or two will be added to a herd of (say) Ayrshires, in order to maintain the fat content officially required. Maundy, a half-Guernsey, had inherited the Guernsey quality, and we hoped that it would pass also with the quarter of her calf that was still Guernsey. If the calf showed any promise of milk, we planned to keep it for our own " herd." It was our first calf and we were inclined to share Maundy's estimation of it. When we placed before it its first bucket of colostrum (the dark-coloured, sticky milk that a cow gives after calving), it seemed puzzled at the inversion of the natural order. D. immersed her hand and presented a finger to the calf. It took to the finger readily, and with much slopping and snorting the milk was gradually sucked up. Calves (like lambs) have a strange habit of delivering a prodigious upward butt of the head to their mothers as soon as the first fine flow slackens. The whole cow quakes under (or rather over) the impact, and is doubtless persuaded or obliged to let down more milk. Such is the blindness of instinct that a bucket-fed calf transfers this impulse to the bucket, with very different results. Our calf soon learned to drink instead of to suck, and no longer needed a helping finger, but she never learned the futility of banging the bucket. Like any healthy calf she reckoned food the greatest of all good things. Throughout the various milk-ing sounds, which she immediately learned to connect with the approach of food, she capered round in her straw, watering at the mouth, and working herself into a frenzy of expectation. The acme was the ecstatic plunge into the bucket, while her tail wriggled in appreciation. Then came the first horrid doubts as she touched bottom, mounting to a second frenzy, of despair. She banged at the unresponding metal, rasped into every corner, and ran around under the upturned bucket in the hope that one precious drop might somehow collect upon her tongue. When despair had passed into resignation she let us peel the bucket from her head and settled down to the eight-hours' wait for the next event. Such is the life of all bucket calves.

This calf was fortunate and did not long remain a bucket-calf. Though Maundy allowed us to milk three of her quarters readily enough, the difficulty of milking the fourth may be imagined. We persisted in the attempt because the quarter *must* be drained ; if milk is left in a cow she tends to dry up at best, and at worst may develop serious infection. The calf, we reckoned, would be rougher than we were if indeed Maundy allowed her to touch that quarter at all. More probably she would kick her away from it. However, we became convinced that, despite the pain we had to inflict at milking time, we were not emptying the quarter. On the advice of neighbours we put the calf and cow together again, to their mutual and incredulous delight. At once the plaster vanished and the stitches " gave." The two faces of the cut healed separately, leaving an opening that by-passed the milk valve. The result was a touching demonstration of the biological side of affection. Whenever she went all sentimental about the calf, as she did regularly and at very short intervals, licking her and speaking to her in the yearning voice reserved for the purpose, milk gushed uncontrolledly through the slot. Some of it the calf swallowed, and most of the remainder was lost. Not quite all, though. The byre-cats quickly discovered this source of manna and stalked Maundy open-mouthed and waiting. They even leaped at the source, but she reacted vigorously. There is astonishing force in the flick of a cow's hind heel.

We named the calf Prima.

Finding names for beasts is always difficult. You may re-name Maggie as Achbeg Choice X, but never an extra drop will that put in the bucket. Yet it seems too arbitrary to take names from a hat. Like others, we called in association. There were at various times in our three years Ruby the red cow, Carrie from Lochcarron and Polly from Ullapool. Cheetah, Jean and Maundy brought their names with them. It is quite common to name a bought cow after her former owner. I used to wonder what visitors made of innocent remarks like, " There's Miss MacHeather come back for the bull," or " Daddy, come quickly, Lady MacBracken is calving in the bog." Prima represented a faint hope of system carried on in Katey, our fourth calf, Seppie the seventh, and Octavia the eighth—the last quickly altered to Caesar when he proved to be a bull calf after all. The sequence broke down with the others : Nicky and Noel born about Christmas, Walker who was born on the hill and immediately walked the half-mile home ; and various others.

Achbeg, as has been said, was different from most crofts in that we sold milk. Before describing the general pattern of Highland stock-rearing I must return to the distinction between suckers (cows that are allowed to suckle their calves) and house-cows (which are not). Very roughly it is the distinction between beef and milk. Probably advances in technique will eventually enable farmers to control the sex of their young stock in advance, but at present one of his endless perplexities is the fact that Nature sends male and female—whether calves, lambs, chicks or anything else—in roughly equal numbers. A type of cow may be bred for milk until the unfortunate beast is hardly more than a walking bag. But her male calves will be worth almost nothing—I have seen bonny brown calves sold in the ring for the price of a packet of cigarettes—and her own carcase will make poor eating when she is dropped from the herd. At the other extreme, a type may be bred for beef until the cows have not enough milk to bring up their young. Cheetah had this defect. As a source of milk for the house she was useless. Some friends recommended us to make a sucker of her since she might in these more natural circumstances produce more milk, enough for a calf; others were doubtful. There would need to have been considerable improvement; no calf would thrive on the milk she contributed to the bucket after the first month or so of a lactation. Some experts believe that the poll Angus and certain other beef-breeds have already overspecialised themselves into this predicament. There is a further complication : while dairy farmers hope for heifer calves, beef farmers hope for bull calves. By no means all the females will be needed for replenishment of the herd, and there is no practicable way of inducing a heifer calf to give her whole mind to beef production, as there is with the male. She will later on be ramping around the fields, a nuisance to herself and others, when she should be quietly making flesh of grass. Hence the heifer calves fetch poorer prices. Whenever a calf was due in the Glen we all hoped that it would be a black bull calf—black, as evidence of poll Angus breeding, and bull for the reason given. There were odd runs of luck. We knew a man who lost considerably because fate seemed to have only heifers for his byre ; and there was another man who, wanting to build up his own herd, could manage nothing but bulls. It is not easy to take a calm, statistical bird's-eye view of your tenth bull-calf in succession, and I do not wonder at the former hold of witchcraft.

In addition to the beef breeds and the milk breeds, there are dual-purpose breeds. Whether they get the best of both worlds or the worst of both worlds is debated wherever farmers stand at street corners.

On a croft milk is needed for the family, but beef is the source of cash income. Transport is a difficulty and there are few concentrated markets for milk, even if the local custom were not against milk selling. Butter is made for the house, and an excellent cheese called crowdie ; occasionally, too, the more familiar types of cheese ; but imported cheese and butter are normally sold at prices with which British farmers cannot begin to compete.

Thus the main output of the croft is beef, and especially calves. As with sheep, the alternation of winter dearth and summer plenty determines the whole rhythm of work. In summer there is a glut of grazing. Farms like Achbeg have, in addition to the parks put aside for grazing, an abundance of rough grass and heather on the hill ground, and the tenants of holdings without rough-grazing can usually make some arrangement with a neighbour. It is in autumn, when the grass dies down, that the pinch comes. From then until the grass grows again the beasts must be given straw and hay to keep them going, and the chief function of the arable is to provide this winter fodder. The more breeding cows can be carried through the winter, the more calves there will be for sale next year. A winter-calving cow means winter milk for the children, but she cannot make milk without straw. She may devour the fodder that would have carried two spring calves through the lean months. Hence calves are in general timed for early spring. A sucker calf does much better than a bucket calf receiving the same quantity of milk ; partly because it helps itself to innumerable small feeds and not just to two or three swilling bellyfuls in the day, and partly, I imagine, because it is happier. A mother after all is considerably more than a fount of bodily nourishment. Twins do not thrive on poor grazing. Later on we did try the experiment of putting two calves on to Ruby, when we were obliged to make her into a sucker. They seemed to be doing well enough, but when I saw them in the truck along with Donald's and especially with a handsome broad-backed calf of Gordon's, I was startled at the difference. The verdict of the ring was interesting. The two calves at six months brought in exactly what we should have received by selling one at the age of three weeks and leaving the other to absorb Ruby's undivided attention.

Sometimes a calf is sold at three weeks old, if the cow's milk is needed for the house ; or it may be fed from the bucket wholly or partly on milk, the balance of

milk going to the house. Some calves will be kept over
the first winter, to be sold later as stirks (beasts in their
second year), or sold later still as calving heifers, or kept
in the herd altogether, but most are sold in the first
autumn. At this time the crofter and his wife must make
some anxious decisions. Just how many of their beasts
dare they keep ? If they overestimate the content of their
stacks, there may be seven lean kine staggering around
the croft to shame them before the grass comes. If they
underestimate, the cattle will come through fat and smiling,
but the chance of an extra calf or two will have been
thrown away, and with it, perhaps, the chance of a holiday
for the family, or some more urgent necessity.

A further use is made of the summer flush of grass.
Stirks or cows are bought in in the spring, grazed for some
months, and sold at the back end, but this is no game for
a beginner. Everything turns on a sound judgment of
cattle beasts and a good forecast of the market. Without
skill and experience the undertaking would be the shortest
road to bankruptcy ; for those who have the qualification
it is an exciting gamble with the promise of fair profit, a
chance of big gains, and a risk of heavy losses should
anything go wrong with market. The prediction of
market prices is an engrossing study, since one factor
involved is necessarily a guess of other people's predic-
tions, and there is scope for ingenious theorising. A
Government subsidy of £4 was offered on beasts grazed
on the hills day and night for a minimum period, one
cause of the poor condition of the hills being the lack
of grazing, treading and dunging from cattle. The subsidy, however, did not form a complete insurance to
summer grazers : in their eagerness competing spring
buyers sometimes bid each other up more than £4 beyond
the true market value of a beast, and then there were long
faces in the autumn. But, of course, the £4 came to rest
somewhere, and usually where it was well enough needed.

For our part, we were hoping to put a few hardy
cattle on our hill, Highlanders, Galloways or possibly a

cross. They stay out throughout the winter and need wonderfully little help. A farmer friend of ours found that his Galloways came for their daily sheaf for a few weeks only, during the very worst of the weather, and for the rest they looked after themselves. There would have been calves to sell, without the speculative risk of summer buying. We never managed to find animals suited to our shelterless hill, and were glad instead to have some of Donald's cattle on our hill in summer. It was a good bargain on both sides : Achbeg had all the gain of fertility and Donald could buy in slightly more head of cattle.

Our problem was partly different because of our milk sales. We were able to sell milk only because the regulations governing the dimensions of byres, the materials, ventilation, washing arrangements, etc., did not apply to farms selling under three gallons a day in our district. If modernised buildings alone were permitted, there would be no milk at all there ! Our byre had rough walls, a cobbled floor with an impossible grip (or dung channel), rafters for the storage of hay, and many other shortcomings. Above all, the midden was straight opposite the door. We did not bother unduly about the cobwebs aloft, but took a good deal of trouble about clean udders, utensils and hands. I think we were reasonably successful in keeping the milk clean ; at any rate we were congratulated on the length of time it " kept " in thundery weather —though I don't know what bacteriological tests might have shown.

It would have been easy enough to find a sale for far more than three gallons a day by going a little farther afield, and we came to think that this would be the best line of development for Achbeg. We therefore asked an official to inspect the byre and make recommendations. Investigation showed, however, that the outlay would be heavy and the returns uncertain. Omitting all unessentials, and allowing nothing for my labour, the cost of alterations would have run into hundreds of pounds. Had we been sure we should stay on at Achbeg we might have taken the risk, but we were not sure, nor could we ask the landlords, the Forestry Commission, to take it for us. Our calculations might prove mistaken. We should, for instance, have to run a motor-cycle combination for delivery, or alternatively to accept the wholesale price only, which was far lower than our 4d. a pint, and it was difficult to allow for the exact effect of this change in costs. The experiment had already been tried on a larger scale not far away by a gentleman-farmer who was much loved and respected for his unusual sense of responsibility in these matters, and on his authority said to be unremunerative. We therefore abandoned the plan, deciding to keep as near to the three-gallon limit as conditions would allow. (How funny three gallons must sound to a dairy-farmer!) To some extent we fell in with the customary solution of the problem of glut and dearth, but we also had to keep up a minimum supply of milk through the winter. One result was an extreme instability in our own larder. In summer we had, like others, plenty of milk to set for butter, but we were the first to have to fall back on powdered or tinned milk for our tea. Before we left Achbeg a customer said that she had not had to go elsewhere for winter milk since we had become her supplier, and, compliments being so rare, we make the most of this one.

It might be thought that maintaining an even flow of milk is the easiest thing in the world : with four cows, you just cause one to calve each season, and, *voilà*, a level supply. But anyone who has tried it knows better. It is hard enough with a fair-sized herd, in which accidents have a chance of evening out ; with a small herd it needs more luck and more judgment than are vouchsafed to mortals. You plant kale to keep up the winter supply, and the rabbits devour it overnight. You plan to bull Maundy in August, and in June she leaps a fence and helps herself. You count Ruby safely bulled in April, and in October there she is asking to be allowed a fresh start. You keep back one cow to be bulled in winter, and not a glimmer of co-operative interest does she show from one equinox to the other. And failing any other obstacle, two "quarters" of your winter cow go as hard as a brick, the vet looks glum, and you must blame it all on a streptococcus. It is useless to hope that you will avoid misfortunes; the most that can be asked is that different misfortunes may cancel out.

In addition to all the ordinary difficulties we had one unknown to the farmer in more populous areas, and perhaps this chapter can best finish with an account of a winter journey undertaken in the interest of a level milk supply. For there is little to say about the cattle work of the first summer, which went smoothly enough after the first mishap. We milked in the mornings, not at 5 a.m., in desperate haste to catch a morning lorry, but at a perfectly human (some might say a shameful) hour, according to the work in hand. Our good resolution to keep to a fixed evening time for milking soon yielded to the pressure of circumstances. Cheetah found many ingenious ways of getting into the growing corn, and Maundy, when she escaped one evening with her calf, gave us an anxious search by starlight among the deep drains of the boggy ground towards Braientra. But such events are the small change of farming life.

Our special difficulty was that the Department bull went away for wintering. There might by good luck be a bull at Pockton or across the water at Lochcarron, but more likely a long and pleasant trip with the cow was unavoidable. One such trip is fresh in my mind, as it occurred much later in the story—only last winter. Perhaps a short account of it will serve to illustrate just how remote our work sometimes was from the standards of the Census of Industrial Production, and just how completely the business of living can still be mixed up with that of earning a living.

We wanted Marie, a recent purchase, to calve the following December, and one Saturday in March she showed a complaisant inclination. Jumbo, the Depart-

ment bull, was not due back for a while yet; there was
no bull at all nearer than Ardelve, where Kenny McE.
had one of his own. Ardelve it must be. Accordingly
I took the goad of propulsion in my right hand and the
halter of restraint in my left, like a figure in some allegory,
and set off for Ardelve with Marie. She travelled well,
knowing the intention. Before starting she resolutely
declined to drink, but soon developed an interest in the
roadside puddles. I led her aside to a burn of fast-sliding
water in peat. The concave of her face scooped up a wash
almost to her ears, and she hadn't the sense to face downstream. Her drink was a series of hurried plunges. I
glanced over my shoulder, to see our house shining through
a fragment of rainbow. Snow still gleamed on the higher
tops. There were showers, but bright sun, a stinging breeze
and the elevation were exhilarating. Glen Udalein, along
the edge of which the road runs, is as bare and soothing
as any that I know. During the miles between the climb
up and the climb down we saw no living creature but
moorland birds and sheep. Buzzards fought in the blue
sky. The sheep, now heavy in lamb, glanced up from
their grazing but were too wise to run from a man with
a cow. Their earmarks told me when I passed from one
grazing to another—first a left quarter, later two right
back-bits, and finally a hole in the right. They rarely
stray far off their own ground, and shed themselves out
at a whistle.

There is a window-like view of Kintail before the long
slope down to Loch Alsh. I gave Marie a rest here while
I wondered about the virginal quality of the Five Sisters
and the Jungfrau. But she too was thinking her own
thoughts. The west wind must have brought her a sniff
of the cattle at Auchtertyre for she set off at a double.
I had meant to take a short cut, but had hardly more
control over the course of events than a dinghy behind
a launch. At the foot of the hill I had to persuade her to
turn down-wind; that is, away from the engrossing scent.
She dug in her heels, all four of them. The halter gave

way to the stick, to our common discomfiture, until a lowing cow somewhere to the east came to my rescue. Kenny MacE. left the turnips he was sorting and took me in for a cup of tea and a chat. A whitewashed Church, the largest in the district, stands near his farm. It will seat a thousand. McE.'s father told him of times when hundreds of worshippers had stood outside the crowded church; to-day, it shelters a few score of people only. And in Glen Udalein, where there are now only the faint marks of former cultivation and not a single cottage, a bugle would once summon sixty-five young and able men from their sixty-five households.

Marie was more sedate on the return journey. The shadows in the valleys crept towards the cliff-tops, and the browns and olive greens of Glen Udalein slowly darkened towards indigo. After the clean wilderness of the moor, the clean homeliness of our Glen, with a few lights and a burst of late song from the blackbirds. We were tired, both Marie and I, but content. We had travelled some sixteen miles. The object of our quest is more precious than empires, and its volume, I believe, about one hundredth of one thousandth of one millionth of a cubic inch.

In purely economic terms, a very small return, for so many man-hours of effort which I would not willingly have missed. Many hikers did just the same trip for pleasure, some of them in no better company. And at least we had the promise of a winter calf for our trouble. Our friend, Charlie McC., had more cause to grumble. He took a cow over three separate times, missing a day's work in the Forestry on each occasion, before she held the service.

And then she slipped her calf.

CHAPTER V

" The hoote somer hadde maad his hewe all broun."
CHAUCER—" Prologue."

At first, we had neither horse, cart nor harness. Hearing that some goods for us had arrived at the station, soon after we had moved in, I went over to Achmore to borrow Donald's horse, in much the frame of mind in which one might approach a bank manager for a loan without security.

" Take him whenever you need him," said Donald.

" Is he quiet ? " I asked. " I'm no bronco-buster."

" Quiet ? Dicky would stand though you took out his tonsils."

This wasn't quite true; when Dicky needed a dose later on Donald took the usual precaution of gagging him with a bit of stick; but there can seldom have been a horse of whom it was more nearly true. It would not much worry me to see infants playing under his belly (as I have indeed seen them playing under a South Devon bull without harm). Nobody knew quite how old Dicky was, but he must have been round about thirty and was still up to a full day's work at the grubber. He sized me up at a glance—a horse doesn't live so long without learning a good deal about human nature. He did in fact work not unwillingly for me, but always as something of a favour. Often later Donald and I were perched on a cart behind Dicky. For me he would do a couple of miles an hour or so. Donald had only to take the reins from me, with not so much as a word or a gesture, for Dicky to show quite a turn of speed. Despite his age, he had a useful and uncommon gait, between walking and trotting, that halved the time taken in " travelling empty " when work was urgent. It may be what is called a jog-trot.

As for the borrowing, Donald was in earnest, and we soon settled down to mutual borrowing and lending until it became quite hard to recall what belonged to whom. John's implements and Donald's had together formed a set. Thus we needed to buy only a set of spike-harrows, chains, a Sellars M.P. plough, a grubber and a few others. The capital cost to each of us was halved—and the area that must be searched for a forgotten tool or implement was doubled. Borrowing has its disadvantages. When you want to make an early start the mower may be here, the blades there, the traces somewhere else, the spanner lent, and the file lost. (Though I do not believe in letting tools lie rusting, I was quite as lax as anyone else. Somehow the work and the weather make orderliness more trouble than it is worth.) In addition Prince may be grazing in the Triangle below the Falls and Dicky driven by the midges to the highest corner of the field towards Strome. But there are also great advantages provided the objects communally used are not communally owned. If " loan oft loseth both itself and friend," far more so does a jointly-owned tractor.

Achbeg and Achmore, I was told, had always worked together. It could hardly be otherwise. Most field-work calls for two horses, and the one-horse farm is a good symbol of the social tie based on economic need. If the tenants of the Big Field and the Little Field ever quarrelled in the past, as I suppose they did at times, there must have been ample fuel to keep the quarrel warm. In our time, the march fence between the two stretches of hill-ground was in need of weeks of repair work. I have an idea the hoggs and gimmers used it for hurdling practice when in the mood for a frisk. But in this respect as in all others there was so much to be gained (quite apart from the intrinsic value of neighbourliness, which is the same everywhere) from working together, that we let the flocks mingle. In the nature of the work there was every inducement to be friendly.

For the moment there were two horses available as Donald had temporarily a mare called Maggie, but we could not go on without a horse of our own indefinitely. We must find a horse, and the right horse. Where the cattle, sheep and poultry merely let matters take their course, there are two creatures, the horse and the dog, that join in active partnership with their owner. We were very lucky with both.

Experience had taught me some kinds of horse I did not want. I did not want a somnolent schemer like Nick on the Island; nor a stamping brute like Tommy in Argyll, who recalled better days as a post-horse, took every incline at the double, and held me in utter contempt. Nor yet a stripling like Treasure in Inverness, who was apt to lie down and roll in the chains. What I did want was a horse young enough to enjoy his work but old enough to have forgotten foalish pranks; heavy enough to split drills alone if the need arose, yet not a voracious feeder; wise enough to put me right yet too friendly to exploit my innocence; and of a size to pair well with Dick. The reputation of horse-dealers is a by-word, and a tender lamb among the lions I should have been in a sale-ring. But we found our perfect horse, and through a salesman—one recommended to me by one of our neighbours.

Donald went down with me to get him off the train. There Prince stood in the horse-box, light chestnut in colour, with a gentle, welcoming look in his eye, yet proud and handsome as a beast in his prime should be. We surveyed him from the neat broad hooves to the alert ears. He was a garron of $15\frac{1}{2}$ hands. I took it for granted that he was two or three years older than the rising seven given as his age; though I could not check this from his teeth. (There would have been no cause for offence in my looking a gift horse in the mouth as I had no idea what to seek there.) His movements in walking on the road were clean and stylish. He could also walk at a good pace, no small gain on a scattered farm where so

Grubbing. Prince and Dick in the spring-tooth harrows, with Meallan in haze beyond.

Achbeg steading. Ramshackle sheds made from railway sleepers supplement the more permanent buildings.

Crofters' strips. Each croft has scattered strips, as in medieval farming. The view is from Achbeg hill.

much time is spent in travelling. He behaved perfectly in all kinds of harness, and with a quiet mind I let the approval period of three days expire.

Prince spent several days wearing tracks along two fences of his field and a patch at the corner, where he stood gazing towards the railway and his former home, until new loyalties were established. He had obviously been a crofter's horse, for whenever he saw a white apron in a doorway or at a window he approached in the expectation of a " piece " (snack).

For the three years that I had him Prince was a pleasure to work with. (Every horse-owner, I expect, considers his horse about perfect.) His only defect was " not his fault " —a skin that was not thick enough to protect him from the West Coast flies and midges. On a bad day he endured agonies from these pestilential creatures. He swelled into little bumps, became restive and was inclined to make unbidden for the cool silent darkness of the stable, cart and all. Prince cost a great deal of money, so much that I have an idea some knowing person forced up the bidding, but we never grudged a penny of it. By the time we came to sell him his known qualities brought in plenty of local enquiries, and his daily loss in value through the period amounted to a few pence only : no great price for the use of a good horse.

We did, however, make one financial error after buying him. It was worrying to have so much money walking on four legs. He might break one of them. Amongst the least pleasant of my early memories is that of standing with a morbid crowd to watch the destruction of a mare who had broken her leg. I shut my eyes and waited wretchedly for the bang that never came, because the instrument I took to be a gun was a humane killer. Or again Prince might fall into a bog. In Argyll I was leading a Clydesdale on harmless-looking ground on a bitter January day when the bridle was snatched from my hand, his head was snorting at my knee and he himself was shoulder-deep in a bog. The green sward had been a mere crust. The poor horse

E

did flounder his way out and was led shivering to the stable. To reduce the risk of pneumonia my employer emptied half a bottle of whisky into a bucket, added warm water and bran, and placed it before him. He sucked it down (or up ?) like any practised Scot. No harm ensued, but I have been over-cautious on soft ground ever since.

So we insured Prince against " death only from accident or disease." Now accident and disease are the only causes of death I can think of other than suicide, which horses leave to their betters. Hence the premium must be calculated in the knowledge that the " risk " is a certainty. Apart from the profit and expenses of the company, the premium takes the place of depreciation if you carry on until the horse eventually dies, as die he must, when a new horse can be bought with the money repaid. Over a short period, however, the premium duplicates the loss in value : when you sell your horse alive he fetches less, and the insurance payments have gone for ever. There was also a supplementary charge (imposed no doubt by actuaries who had in mind the horses in Piccadilly rather than those on Strome Brae) because he was employed for coal-carting. But we refused to pay this the second year and the third year we let the policy lapse. (Its terms excluded death from grass-sickness, which is a scourge where it strikes but is almost unknown on the West.)

Nell, our sheepdog, was as good as Prince in her smaller way, but she came later.

One by one we picked up the implements and tools we needed, including a light coup-cart (or tip-cart), with harvest frame to fit. We were very glad to have it, but I always felt ashamed of it beside Donald's. His was panelled and spoke-shaved for lightness, its wheels were broad and large for use on soft, rough ground, and the " dish " of them was just right, so that each spoke was vertical when it bore the weight. Ours was flimsy and unworkmanlike by contrast, and the product of a different age with different ideals. It was only five quarters lighter and carried much less in its box. We turned the differences to account, using Donald's for field work and ours for lighter road work where possible.

It was beginning to feel like a farm, with sheep, cows, a horse and a cart, but for some time there was an important lack. We had no harness. Only by borrowing could I link the horse to the cart. My attempt to improvise deepened my wonder at the ingenuity and simplicity of cart harness. Perfect rigidity where needed is combined with perfect flexibility where needed. The horse's spine can point almost at five o'clock while he grazes in a ditch, or at one o'clock while he tries the hazel leaves above; he can trot, gallop and back and do almost anything but sit; and through it all the living horse and the dead cart maintain a perfect harmony of motion. It is just one of those many small perfections that give a glimpse of generations of thought, experiment and adaptation.

After our settling in I set to preparing pyramids and racks for haymaking. Perhaps I may mention in passing, what I did not know in my pedagogic days, that by far the most important crop in the world is grass (grazed direct, or made into hay, silage and dried grass) and the most important farm product in the world is milk. The latter, according to a report of the Raw Materials Committee of the late League, is about twice as valuable as wheat, rice, maize, oats and all other cereals put together. But I do not know quite how an Indian peasant's rice is measured against a Hebridean crofter's milk when neither of them can do anything but consume it.

Like all the others in the Glen we were planning to make clover hay and meadow hay. In former days the oats grown provided the porridge, brose and oatcake for which Scotland is famous, and traces of the mills can be found; but now, apart from potatoes, very little is grown for direct consumption or for sale as a cash crop. The main purpose of the arable, as I have already said, is to provide winter keep for the largest possible number of cattle. It might almost be said that a crofter spends the summer preparing for the winter, and the winter holding on for the summer again. Ley farming, which is much recommended in England now as a means of restoring and retaining fertility, has always been the basis of Scottish farming. The plough travels round the farm to every park that will take it. When the grass or ley is ploughed, corn ("ley corn") is nearly always the first crop taken off. "Corn," of course, refers to the most common cereal in a district, which here is oats. Next year follow potatoes, sometimes with turnips or kale. In the third year corn is sown on the ground which by now is well cleared of turf and weeds. In Argyll it was called "red ground corn," in Ross-shire "black-ground corn." Grass-seed is sown along with the black-ground corn seed, so that in the fourth year there is a crop of grass and clover, usually mown for "clover hay." The ground will be left under grass for perhaps a couple of years more, grazed if the family can afford to nurse their ground, otherwise mown again. The second-year grass retains much grass of the varieties originally sown, apart from the Italian rye-grass, which is an annual, but in the third and subsequent years natural grasses are becoming prominent. Hay taken off now is called meadow hay. Rashes also creep in in the West Highland climate. Eventually the ley is ploughed again, some six to eight years after the original ploughing, and the whole round is started once more. On fields which for one reason or another do not plough well, meadow hay only will usually be harvested.

Accordingly, in the terms of our lease, one crop we had to take over at valuation was the sloping clover field at the farther end of the farm, beyond the Falls. Surprisingly, our fields had no old names that we could discover, and this field we had to name for ourselves as the Dalfearn Acre. There was also a long narrow strip of meadow hay beside the road, close to the house, in the Road Park. For a fair number of years it had been yielding excellent hay crops, we were told, but it was now feeling the strain. Sorrel, plantains and other weeds were becoming abundant. It would have been better to graze it as a preliminary to re-ploughing, but first, we needed the hay, and, second, there was no fence between it and the adjacent strips bearing corn and potatoes.

Haymaking was to be our main preoccupation for some time to come, apart from the struggle with maggot, but other work was, of course, going forward at the same time. The effort to stem the tide of weeds on the potato-strip can only be mentioned here ; and there was also the patch of fallow ground we had taken over, below the potatoes. The Road Park, as I have just said, was worked in three strips, that ran from the house down to the river. The first had meadow hay, the second black-ground corn, and the upper half of the third potatoes. The lower half of the last had been ploughed and harrowed, ready for kale, but it was difficult ground because of its steepness. There was a warp in the field that became steeper as you crossed the three strips and it finally became quite unmanageable where the river ran in a half-gorge. Birch and hazel had been allowed to remain there for shelter.

Dunging, grubbing and harrowing the patch were breathless work for man and horse. I thought many times that the cart was about to tip sideways on the slope, and Prince's one desire was always to get back on to the level ground.

Immediately on arrival we had prepared and sown a seed-bed of kale in the garden. The first sowing was ready for transplanting, and we intended to start dibbling the plants in one wet day soon. But there was the danger from rabbits. Many lived in the wood, and I suspect that others followed Tom's sheep and lambs across the river bed in dry weather. I therefore wrote to an ironmonger for four rolls of rabbit netting and was told a Committee permit was needed. I wrote to the Committee and was told to say it all again on a form. I did so and was informed that the month's quota of permits had been issued but I should get one later on. Meanwhile the kale plants were choking one another in the seed-beds and we resolved to go ahead. On a really drenching afternoon I lined out part of the field and dibbled away. The chief advantage of my mackintosh was that the stream of water inside was always a little warmer than the stream outside. By tea-time thousands of little kale plants were drinking in the rain in tidy rows ; and by morning there was not one leaf left—hardly even a stalk to show where the kale had been. Discouraged I decided to wait for the netting before trying again. Eventually three rolls of netting did arrive, too late to be of use. Three, in any case, would have left a 30-yard gap with nothing to restrain the rabbits but a general sense of fair play. We found a hundred uses for the rolls of netting but they were destined never to keep rabbits out of our kale.

Nevertheless we were on the whole little troubled by controls or by form-filling and the information asked for on the forms was obviously necessary for the Government. Their chief fault was inflexibility. The same form, requiring 159 answers, 63 of them in duplicate, was sent to the Duke of Sutherland and to any poor widow with a pension and three hens. Isabella, an octogenarian neighbour of ours, used to bring us her forms to fill in. She had a small patch of corn, a smaller patch of potatoes, and a few hens. We derived much amusement together from the questions.

" How many bulls have you, Isabella ? "

" What would I, that haven't so much as a heifer calf, be wanting with a bull ? "

" How many acres of onions ? "

" Onions indeed ! "

" Any unbroken horses ? "

" The questions they will be asking."

" Did you measure your strips ? "

" No, but you've seen them."

" We'll put ' Ocular survey '."

(We got away with ocular survey as the mode of computation.)

There was one matter into which we could not follow the official mind. Isabella had a ewe on her own ground in addition to one on ours. Her 4s. subsidy did not arrive. I wrote asking the reason. The reply was that there were two reasons : the ewe had not appeared on her December return, and *the sheep in question did not appear to be in regular age classes* !

But with a guaranteed sale for our wool and potatoes at guaranteed prices, several direct subsidies, other indirect subsidies, and very little intervention in the running of the farms, we had little cause to carp at bureaucrats.

In a certain book about English farming the hay is said to be cut on Monday, turned with a swathe-turner on Tuesday, and stacked on Wednesday. It may be sometimes. Sometimes, I know, it is alternately washed and bleached for long enough between cutting and stacking. In the west of Scotland farmers have devised ways of outwitting the climate which entail much work, but which, with any luck, yield excellent hay, better than I have seen in the south. Hay is not the stringy colour of the outside of a hay-stack, or should not be ; it is an appetizing bluey-green and has a smell faintly suggestive of wild thyme.

The most common method is by way of " coils " (or " quoils "). The grass is cut, whether by mower or by scythe, and turned. When both sides of the swathe have dried slightly the grass is raked into windrows and forked into small beehive shapes, the coils. It now offers less surface to the action of the sun and the rain, and is largely clear of the layer of relatively stagnant air that seems to lie close to the ground. Given a good breeze and no rain, the hay in a day or two can be shaken out and rebuilt in considerably larger coils. There is much skill in the rapid building of light coils that will shed the rain and not list over in the wind. The process may be repeated until the hay is in large stamp-coils, built by a worker who rises as the coil mounts. Throughout, the aim is to keep the hay in the largest possible coils that will not heat. An old sack may be tied to shed the rain from the point of the stamp-coil, and thereafter the hay can be left for carting at any convenient time. The weather, however, is not usually so well disposed. Showers, heavy or light, will increase the amount of shaking out and re-coiling needed, and the final stages are carried on indoors. The hay is forked thinly or thickly according to its condition, on to diagonal racks in the barns, and then packed into a heap or "bing" in some convenient covered spot. Donald was lucky in having a huge old barn with great areas of slatted window and wicker-work. Its beautifully curved beams and its general proportions recalled a village church. In this barn he lashed together a number of larch-poles to form a very large "clichy" (as the rack is called) and still had room for his hay and corn "bings." A farmer would deduce much about local conditions from a glance at our barns and at our small round stacks.

A second traditional method, common in the similar conditions of Norway also, is to build the hay lightly on wire fences, either the ordinary field boundaries or fences specially constructed on the spot. Provided there is a slight breeze and the fences are well sited, grass can be cut and dried in steady rain. Here again there is much skill in rapidly loading the grass so that it neither compacts itself nor tumbles off.

A third method resembles that practised by peasants in Lombardy and other parts of Europe. Portable structures are erected on the field to receive the hay within 24 hours of cutting : it can, if there has been good drying and the sky has a doubtful look about it, be loaded even on the day of cutting. A skeleton pyramid is the usual structure, formed by four 8-ft. poles loosely hinged or tied at the apex. A few rounds of wire or stack-rope keep the centre clear. When the hay has been raked into rings, a pyramid is placed in the centre of each. Hay is forked in light heaps that mount the four legs. At a height of a foot or two it becomes possible to bridge the space between the legs. Thereafter the hay is added in rounds that must knit together yet never pack. Now comes the climax of the operation : the hay round the legs is pulled away and is forked on to the top. If you are a beginner, the structure

collapses at this point and you start again; but once you
have acquired the knack the whole thing rests squarely
on its four wooden legs and not a wisp of the hay is
touching the ground. A cap is made of longish hay well
shaken so that the strands point all ways to shed the rain,
and gently lowered on to the apex. Two crossed ropes
are thrown over, and you can forget about the hay until
it is cured and ready for carting—unless a real gale inter-
venes. The pyramids seldom overturn, however, and can
be tent-pegged if the need arises.

And if a shower catches the workers unawares, as it
very frequently does, rows of trim wig-wams stand ready
to offer shelter. No rain ever penetrates. They are lovely
places for children to play in and sooner or later I imagine
the bees will discover them for swarming.

It was in making a score of these pyramids, then, and
in fitting up the barn, that I occupied the first lull. Our
barn being much smaller than Donald's, I adopted a
different arrangement of clichies. A large single rack
filled the north end of the barn, and a double-tiered rack
filled half the south end, the remaining quarter being left
clear for elbow-room. There were extra devices for
making use of spare corners and the rafters too could
be filled. All the racks folded into the roof when not in
use, to release the space for other purposes.

In order to force the grass on and make use of the
better weather that can be hoped for in the early summer,
I had sown sulphate on both pieces. Before they were
ready, however, I scythed grass in two nearby gardens
and put it up on pyramids, in order to learn the method.

Our main cutting, both at Achbeg and at Achmore, was
to be done with a mowing machine, in the ownership of
which we had taken over a one-third share from John. It
was a remarkable mower in several ways, not least in a
complete immunity to depreciation. The three farms of
the upper Glen had bought it jointly for £15 long before,
and at a change of tenancy the incoming tenant always
bought a one-third share for £5. When, at the sound of

the trump of doom, its rusty components reassemble from a dozen scrapheaps, it will still be worth £15.

It might more properly be called a course in mechanical engineering than a mower, for I believe we spent more hours in contorted postures under, beside and within it than upon the driving seat. There was movement in it in many spots where none should be, and all too often none at all where movement would have been most welcome. As heard by D. in the kitchen, a typical day's mowing might run like this. First the clank of the machine on the road. A pause for decisions, then " Come up Princie, come up Dicky." A few seconds of hesitant clicking cut short abruptly. " Dicky, you black scoundrel, that was you." Clicks from the free-wheel mechanism as the mower was tugged clear of the grass for the blade to be freed. " Now, come away, horses. Dicky, Princie." Clickety-clickety-click and a bang. " Oh, Princie, Princie, you'll break my heart." A dozen such starts and stops, and then a long silence, if the buzzing of a million flies could be called silence. Taps of metal on metal and puzzled voices. " Head up, horses, head up, Prince." The silence might go on to dinner-time, tea-time, supper-time or bed-time, with or without short spells of faltering clicking. Sooner or later, that day or next, a voice would say, " Well, well, so that's what it was. I wonder the thing ever went at all." Finally, when additions, subtractions and adjustments were all made, there might (or might not) be a half-hour or with luck a half-day of the music of mowing. Just how musical is that sound nobody knows who has not lain under a mower, with a cloud much bigger than a man's hand coming up in the west.

The main trouble was that the machine was apt to jam as soon as the blade encountered anything thicker than " grass you could see a flea jump in," to quote a Skye man. Sometimes it worked for as long as we kept the horses at the double, charging like Boadicea's steeds in a murderous, rattling onslaught. Sometimes old draw-chains wreathed on the wheels gave the extra grip needed but they always broke and flailed dangerously around. It would be tedious to mention all the troubles we diagnosed, except perhaps the strangest find of all. At some time the wheels had been dismantled, and one had been reassembled with the ratchets of the free-wheel mechanism in reverse ; for years the thing had been running on half its motive power. After this discovery we had several holiday weeks of untroubled mowing, but we ended it by being too clever. With nails, washers and wire we got rid of most of the unwanted play at the joints and it was never the same machine again.

A man's time is reckoned at about ten shillings a day ; but on the critical day, when the red clover flowers have withered and the rye-grass is not yet running to stem and a blue sky and drying wind say, " Now or never for the hay," a day lost may be a ton of hay lost. In the Highland climate it often is now or never. Though I know all too well that you should never spend when you can make do on a croft, I believe that mower was a most extravagant economy.

The weather was very broken through the hay season. Whenever a bright morning gave promise of a fair day we had to decide whether to cut, and how much ; for an acre of sodden grass is an acre of misery. Since there were no wireless weather forecasts at the time we all turned to " Post," the local postman. He lived by the shore (indeed, below the high-water mark, so that he had no rent to pay) and his leisure went into his boat and into fishing. He was thus a close student of the weather. His detractors said that he worked on the formula, " It'll be a fine day— if it doesn't rain," but his advice was much sought after, and many an acre we cut—or didn't cut—on his advice.

For my part, I preferred to cut a little at a time, and get it safely on to sticks before cutting more ; but the whimseys of the mower and the fact that it was only partly mine made planning difficult. And soon an increasing part of my attention was taken up in the search for afflicted sheep. Still, moist weather is as bad for hay as for sheep.

Sometimes the perfect hay day, when it came, had of necessity to be given over to clipping ewes or dipping them to delay further attacks. When the chance came to cut at all, therefore, we usually had to cut more than we could handle if rain came and to hope it wouldn't. But it nearly always did.

Donald and I worked at the hay together. To begin with the mower behaved badly. We started some adjustments that developed into a major operation—that of contriving a substitute for a cracked casting. At length we cut some of Donald's grass, and went on to cut ours at the Dalfearn Acre. The blue sky had long since given way to grey. Before we had finished the field a drizzle had begun—one of those Scottish drizzles that seem to consist of something wetter than water. Next morning D. and I started to put the grass on to a fence, but a good wind came up and we were able to load the pyramids. (For fences will take grass in almost any condition, but not so pyramids.) Mrs. Ferguson came out to help with the pyramids. When the wind dropped towards night the midges came out in their millions. The Highland midge deserves a chapter to itself. I do not know which is the more remarkable, that so much venom can be packed into so small a body, or that so many of the bodies can inhabit space without forming a mist. A Commando told me he would rather go into action than face the midges at their worst—at least he knew what to do when in action. That evening they were at their worst. Mrs. Ferguson brought out some gauze curtains which we wore as veils tucked in at the neck, but the sweat caused by the stuffiness inside the veils seemed just to provide a new element for the midges that had penetrated. In desperation we had to give up, but the weather was kind and we finished next day. It is asking for trouble to leave hay on the ground overnight except in a really good spell.

So the weeks went by, with mowing, scything, raking, forking, loading, unloading, shaking and building. Mrs. McB., Donald's mother, could beat us all at coiling. A number of neighbours helped, busy as they must have been themselves. The bings (indoor stacks) of sweet-smelling hay rose towards the rafters—Donald sprinkled salt on each layer of his for greater safety—but before all the hay was in, the corn was ripe, so much had maggot delayed us. Corn will not wait. The remnant of the grass had to be left until after corn-harvest, by which time it was too thick and tough for the mower. We scythed it and put it on fences, but, with the shorter days and damper winds of October and its over-ripeness, it made very poor hay indeed. I am sorry to say the cattle were eating it with zest before the winter was out.

The clock ceased to matter during those weeks ; everything went according to the state of the weather—the sun, wind, rain and dew—and the state of the hay. At all hours of the day there might be a sudden alarm—" Rain coming in from Skye." Whether it was Donald who had hay spread or ourselves, figures came running out, fork or rake in hand, and some or all of the hay was coiled or bundled on to the cart and tipped under cover. Meal-times were completely erratic, but the womenfolk, who were themselves joining in with haymaking, contrived to find something for all helpers and to bring out unending " fly cups of tea " to the fields. (A cup of tea in this country is quite a hearty snack.) Always there was time for conversation and for good-humoured teasing. The women, especially, conducted a competitive raillery at a speed that left me several moves behind. Without a knowledge of the speakers themselves and others referred to, and without the background of hay, brief glimpses of the sun, and help willingly given, the reader might find the back-chat dull, even if I could recall it. Only odd remarks come back to my mind. One that still amuses me was made by Mrs. McL. Some national figure of great age had recently married a young woman and died on his honeymoon. Commiseration—less for the groom than the bride—had been generally expressed when Mrs. McL. summed up with : " The poor soul !

she had barely the time to open his eyes before they were shut for ever." We also used to discuss the different systems of haymaking. Donald held that in an average year a given amount of trouble would make more good hay on the ground than on sticks, though really bad weather might tilt the balance the other way : we were for the pyramids in either case. Partly is it a difference of temperament.

Our strangest meal came about thus. D. and I were working late to get the last of some hay off the ground. At about ten o'clock Donald, who had been busy elsewhere, saw us and joined in. We forked and chatted. A breeze kept the midges away, there would be no real darkness that night, we were interested in our argument, and nobody felt moved to hurry. The last rope was tied and I glanced at my watch. Exactly midnight. A cuckoo turned in his sleep and cuckooed once. We all went to the kitchen and had a meal called afternoon tea. The previous meal had been midday dinner.

That, admittedly, was exceptional, but the whole nature of the work on a croft makes strict punctuality impossible. You cannot cut seven-eighths of a field and then go in for a meal, nor can you cart a half-load because there isn't time for a whole load. The womenfolk have a poor time of it, therefore ; many a tasty meal must have spoiled in the oven. Perhaps that is why broth, oatcake and scones still make up so much of the diet. A delay of two or three hours is nothing to scones and tea, but to a souffle it is murder. Moreover, the irregularity is demoralising, and I am afraid we were often very late indeed where the excuse was hardly more than nominal. If films and fiction may be trusted, there is a revival of interest in crofting at present. I would advise any girl thinking of marrying a crofter to start straight in with a system of signals, possibly a sequence of coloured flags with graded meanings : " Dinner ready," " Dinner spoiling," " Now or never," and " Off home to Mother."

CHAPTER VI

AUTUMN

" Poor fellow, never joyed since the price of oats rose ; it was
the death of him."—SHAKESPEARE—" Henry IV," Part I.

Knots are really the sailor's speciality, but there are
interesting knots in farming too, and autumn is a season
of knots. Though a good knot is not exactly beautiful,
it has an economy of means and a fitness to purpose that
appeal directly to the mind much as beauty does through
the senses. The difference between a reef knot and a
granny is almost a moral difference.

Bags are tied with an ingenious knot that gives the
same leverage as a slip-knot, yet is easily untied with no
breaking of finger-nails. There is another good knot on
a larger scale, by which the rope over a load of corn is
fixed to the shaft ; it makes great tension possible, is
quickly loosened, and doesn't need to be at the end of
the rope. A cow halter has two small bowlines through
which run the two bigger loops, one over the head and
one round the muzzle. If the cow struggles it tightens
without risk of damage and neither escape nor choking
is possible. Sometimes the small loops are spliced, and so
are the loops for clip-hooks on reins. There is a quick-
release knot for hoisting cows' tails during milking. We
always tied their tails to bits of rope hanging from a line
attached to the rafters. When I was sawing wood behind
the byre one morning I was puzzled by loud creaks from
the roof. I hurried round to find Ruby straining forward
through the door : D. had forgotten to untie her tail
before loosing her. Something snapped, the whole byre
seemed to rattle, and Ruby walked sedately on to the

drinking-pond. I half-expected to see her tail dangling in the byre but it was the rope that had given. After that I was careful always to keep to the quick-release knot. The ropes that hold a tarpaulin on a stack, or keep the point of the stack roof steady, may be fixed in two ways. Sometimes stones are attached. Even fairly light stones hold a sheet surprisingly well in a high wind provided no flapping starts—once that happens, nothing can stand to a real wind. The stone is fixed by a rapid movement during which it is spun through a half-turn. Stones have the advantage that they sink as the hay settles and keep everything taut, but a different system is often more handy. A tail of hay or straw is teased out of the stack, the rope and the tail are twisted together, and the wisp is tucked *under* and back—under, to avoid leading rain into the stack. There are also many clever tricks analogous to knots in the handling of wire. We had a thousand different uses for bits of wire and I find it very hard to understand how humanity ever managed the long slow climb to agricultural civilisation without the aid of cheap wire. But a description of the various devices would be dull. They give pleasure as the solution of a problem only if you have yourself been baffled by the problem.

There is one knot or twist that is tied many thousands of times in September and October on the West, that which holds together a sheaf of corn. A wisp of long straws is placed on the ground, a bundle of corn is laid across it, the ends of the wisp are put together, the band so formed is pulled tight, the sheaf is spun or the ends are screwed, and the screw is doubled back under the band from below. Always from below (again) or there would be a pocket to hold water. It is laborious for the beginner, but is performed at astonishing speed by those who learned the knack of it as children on their parents' crofts. Two scythes, four lifters and one stooker would keep each other going on average ground, though of course the numbers varied according to the crop—and the persons. Mrs. McH. could lift two sheaves to my one, and have

Ducklings. At this stage the hen in charge of them gives up the attempt to understand.

Loading dung. The hens soon gather for the undigested corn.

Home-made roller. It worked well and cost nothing.

Broadcasting corn. The crofts at the head of the Glen stood in an amphi-theatre of planted trees.

spare energy to chivvy the Forestry girls while I was numb and dumb with back-ache. Most people took a pride in their skill at scything, lifting or stooking: Isabella used to tell us she had kept three scythes going in her younger days: " When I was young there was none could come near me," she often said. But I think it must have been a very sparse crop. The stooking is not easy on steep, windswept fields, especially if a beginner has made the sheaves. Four sheaves and no more go to a stook, with a twist of straw to hold the points together. They must be paired for weight and jabbed into the stubble, so that the whole stook stands with an almost Gothic precision of counterpoise. A spiral sprawl will grow out of any latent imbalance as the drying sheaves begin to sag, and then there will be neighbourly quips to face as well as the labour of rebuilding the slippery sheaves. Gordon told me that when he first arrived from the East Coast he stooked his sheaves in the more usual eights or tens, but he found that there was a good reason for local custom. His larger stooks refused to season in the damp air of the West.

A combine-harvester would have made little headway in our fields, supposing it could have reached them at all. In some it would have had no room to turn round; in others it would have settled into the soft earth; and in others again it would have rolled down the slope like a boulder. An enterprising farmer—it was John, our predecessor—had tried a binder on Achbeg, but the draft had proved too heavy for the horses. John " came out " all right on his binder, though he might have lost heavily.

Corn is normally no trouble while it is growing. Potatoes, however, had occupied some of the ground the previous year, and all the little tubers left in the ground were now sending up flourishing green stems. No amount of care at potato-lifting time can clear the ground entirely of tubers. A hard winter frost is needed to finish the work, and the previous winter had been mild. Thus we spent several days pulling at the shaughs, one by one. If the

F

work was monotonous, there were at least the breeze and brilliant sunshine and more larks than I could distinguish. Often the tubers proved to be no bigger than hazel-nuts, yet they sprouted as vigorously as full-sized tubers. Our second piece of black-ground corn, a wet triangular piece below the Falls known as the Triangle, having been under turnips, offered no such problem; nor did the ley corn across the road from the house. This last was in the Two-Acre Park, our only field on the Achmore side of the main road. It had been transferred from Achmore to Achbeg at some recent date; the soil was good, the tilt just sufficient for drainage, there was water for cattle, and there were no awkward corners. In short, it was the best park on the farm, and had already a promising crop on it at the time of the valuation. An incidental advantage was that all its fences, being march fences, were in theory the landlord's responsibility. In reality it made little odds. The Forestry Commission were accommodating landlords in a number of ways, including the repair of internal fences for which the lease held me responsible.

The first corn in the Glen to show signs of yellow was a steep, small field of Mrs. Ferguson's, between our Triangle and Dottacks; she grew corn for hens upon it. Donald and I had spent the morning of the last Saturday in August cleaning up maggoty sheep, and after dinner, with D., we went down to give a hand. I was surprised to find a good number of people already cutting, lifting and stooking, including some from the very head of the Glen. At hay people had helped now and then, as need arose: for corn there was a more systematic turn-out, because corn, as I have said, will not wait. By tea-time the enclosure was terraced with stooks, and Donald and I went back to the sheep.

In addition to the rest of us, some of the Forestry men and Forestry girls used to help, by a very convenient arrangement. They were under no pressure to come, but came willingly. Their wages by the day or half-day, charged to us by the Forestry, represented about our only wages bill. In our whole three years our labour-costs amounted to a few pounds. And, of course, the presence of several eligible spinsters and bachelors on the field was a stimulus to the general battle of repartee.

Next to ripen was a very much larger field of Donald's. The straw should be greenish when cut : the head will ripen sufficiently while the sap dries out in the stook. Corn cut ripe will lose much of the head in handling ; if it is cut too green the threshing later will be very disheartening work. The right moment must be seized—if the weather permits. By September the weather is very unreliable.

Our first day was one of unbroken sunshine and we made the most of it. Donald and two other men in echelon swung rhythmically at the scythes. Usually each swung at his own pace, but occasionally they swung in unison, with a concerted grace not often seen in the more studied movements of ballet. I did the stooking for a while.

" Now then there, no putting them closer by the roadside," a passer-by called from the road.

The women took a swathe each and kept abreast, so that they could talk while they worked, and I caught tantalising snatches as the stooking brought me near or sent me beyond earshot.

" They promised me some cups in Morrison's yesterday." (Morrison, the local ironmonger, had a shop on two floors.)

" Was it on the ground floor or upstairs ? "

" Upstairs. Why ? "

" That's all right. They're said to tell lies on the ground floor and the truth upstairs. Why are you smiling ?"

" I'm thinking it's lucky they haven't a basement."

The rest unfortunately I missed.

At a call from Lizzy, who helped Donald's mother, we all trooped in to dinner. More cutting, lifting and stooking, and then tea in the fields. But the weather was too good to be wasted. While those who had cows to see to or other work went off for a while, the rest of us continued our slow stooping progress across the field, which by now seemed enormous. Dusk fell and we all went in to supper, with tired, aching backs ("Not acres but achers," I reflected when we looked back at the field), pleased that the harvest was now in full swing.

Next day we continued in the same fashion and Prince created a diversion. Having escaped from the field in which he had been grazing he found the open gate of the Two-Acre Park. He sampled the head of a stook, and liked it. When I approached to catch him he cantered off and a rare hunt began. He could snatch a bite without slackening speed, and only when a misguided fancy took him out through the open gate once more did we get rid of him. The Northern Lights were darting overhead when we disbanded.

" A bad sign," said Donald, " it usually means broken weather."

Next day, a Saturday, sheep work intervened—we could delay dipping no longer. And on Sunday the weather broke. Donald had been right.

After a few days of rain, a strong wind dried out the corn and about tea-time Donald again started to cut. Soon there was a line of bowed backs. With the days rapidly shortening we had to work while we had the light, and we made the most of the three or four perfect days that followed. Our own ley corn came next, then some parks along the Glen, and finally the black-ground corn. Two men home on leave joined in the scything. Showers and heavy storms delayed the work. For a while the river was in spate ; branches and foam piled against the flood-gates, and the brown water churned deafeningly over the Falls. And always, when we began to think the corn was lost, a change in the wind would save us.

Normally a mower is not employed in corn because it does not lay the corn so tidily for the lifters as a good scythesman will. In a strip where the spurrey had thinned the corn, however, Donald tried the mower to speed up the cutting. Nobody was sorry when it broke down.

Previously we had been working in a sociable group, within talking distance : now the needs of the machine broke up the party. Because every swathe had to be lifted before the horses came round again, to prevent trampling, we were spaced out, each with his own beat. Instead of working at our own speed we were all racing to clear our stretch before the mower bore down on us again. There was, of course, no compulsion other than the nature of the machine itself, but that was sufficient : the machine dominated the field.

There is a saying that the corn must stand in the field for three Sundays, that is, a good fortnight ; if it is packed or stacked sooner it may heat from the sap that is in the straw and the weeds. It can, however, be built fairly soon into " scruans," solid beehive shapes 6-8 feet high, rather like stamp-coils. The intention is the same as with stamp-coils, to get as much of the material off the ground as possible and to decrease the surface offered to rain without shutting out the air. We preferred an alternative type of scruan that can be built on the wooden pyramids made for hay. It takes longer to build but can often be made within a couple of days of stooking ; moreover *all* the sheaves are off the ground and all the butts are exposed to the wind. The butts are hard to dry, chiefly because of the weeds and grass caught up in them, and care must also be taken over the close-packed corn under the band if the crop has been cut after a shower. When prolonged broken weather keeps the sheaves wet for weeks, not only does the straw become limp and blackish, but tender green shoots spring from the grain itself. Good oats and good fodder can become poor bedding.

Last comes the work of carting to the rick, bing or (most often) the clichy. Carting on steep and stony ground has its hazards, but the loaded cart will tilt surprisingly before it topples. There is much pleasure in building the load. I soon learned to make a reasonably shapely load, given time, but speed is essential where the work is a sprint to beat the next shower. Mr. Hardie, my employer in Fife, claimed that he could build to three or four forks, each fork sending up doubles—and his wrath fell upon anyone who pitched a sheaf wrong end round for building. On our two-wheeled carts care must be taken to keep the weight central—neither " light on the back " (so that the belly-rope is half-lifting the horse into the air), nor so heavy on the back that the horse is struggling under the weight that should be on the wheels. Spoons built a load of such shape that five of us had to hold down the shafts, and my own first load was hardly better. There is also skill in deciding just how high any particular load may be made : too small a load means time lost and too ambitious a load may fall—with or without the cart and the horse, according to the ropes used. Donald and I miscalculated with some corn we were taking up from Dalfearn. At the steep bit of road by the Falls the load on one cart swayed, righted itself and toppled—not luckily, into the river. We went on with what was left, the poverty of the load emphasised by the much larger load in the second cart. Sure enough we met Gordon, whose only comment was : " Mon, mon, have ye nae wheelbarrow ? "

There is beauty in every stage of the corn work—the tall crop, the curving swathe beside the wall of green straw suddenly exposed, the stooks, the neat scruans (very ghostly by moonlight), the movement of the workers ; above all, for those who have worked on the field, the clean expanse of stubble at the end : " Now let it rain if it wants ! "

Whenever the chance offered, then, we snatched one more cartload from the threat of the weather. Sometimes, before Prince was fetched and harnessed, a shower had come on and the chance was past. At other times we worked till darkness and after. The last load of Donald's went into the barn by starlight. A lantern, we found, blinded us rather than helped. We groped for the stooks, and kept up a continuous sound (whether of rustling corn or of conversation) in order to avoid spiking one another with the forks. The buildings were hardly more than starless patches, but we could discern ghostly puffs of mist gliding indifferently across the field. When the last sheaf was in we saw to the horses and hurried in to the bright fire and bright lights of the kitchen. What contentment of mind and body was with us all that evening !

When the corn was dry enough it went straight on to the " bing," but more often it had first to be tucked for a while into the slats of the clichy, or up into the rafters, or in any corner where a good draught would go through it. The barn would be wholly enveloped in delicately-drooping heads of oats—like a dream of harvest festival. Our own small barn was soon packed with corn and there was a good deal more to come in. I did not care to try my hand at making an outdoor stack, which calls for much skill if it is not to heel over when it settles, but Miss Stewart came to our aid. Her little croft, which had been made a good while ago on our Lower Flat by dint of much blasting, carting and levelling, was not being worked that year and she kindly agreed to lend us her barn. The last dozen loads filled it to the roof ; there was just room for the door to open. Every day for a while I went up to see if the corn was heating, because we had been obliged to pack it very wet. I pushed a rake handle in to the centre but could find no cause for alarm. In breezy weather surprising chances can be taken with the corn. John, whose reputation as a rick-builder lived on, at times packed his corn so wet that the other men told him to cap the stack with a chimney. Everyone watched for the steam and smoke and flame, but none came.

In later years we did build stacks in the steading, to reduce the winter carting ; or rather, Gordon built them for us. In order to counteract the dampness of the climate various precautions are taken. A thick layer of brushwood raises the stack well clear of the ground, a wooden tripod keeps an air space up the centre, and a tunnel faces the prevalent wind. The stacks are round and small. A layer of whins is meant to discourage the mice, but as may well be imagined the centre of the stack is much too attractive for them to be put off by a few prickles. With the clear space up the middle for access and the heads of the sheaves close packed to form an inexhaustible larder, the round stacks must be a mouse's idea of heaven in every respect but one, that there is no water. (If there is water, the farmer will regret it.) For the mice the lack is desperate. Often on winter nights, when pouncing winds clawed at the roofs, trees and stacks, I crept out of bed to see that the ropes were holding; and there, on the lee-side, immobile amid all the racket, crouched Puss-ah-puss, the house-cat, laying patient siege. She had only to wait: the mice within were doubtless on a knife-edge between thirst and terror, and thirst would surely win. Farming gives innumerable glimpses of such tiny agonies—and, luckily, of tiny pleasures also.

Our store of corn looked very small when I reflected how long it must last the cattle; but when I thought of working through it sheaf by sheaf with a stick, it seemed a veritable mountain. No travelling thresher ever came our way, and the old horse mills lie rusted and broken. Yet the corn had to be threshed because it served a double purpose. Only the straw goes to the cattle; the head feeds the poultry.

Hitherto I have hardly mentioned poultry. The ration of bought chick-food and hen-food was based on the number of poultry kept at an earlier date, when we naturally had had none. We could therefore do little in the interval between our ingoing and our first harvest, but we kept all the hens we could keep on scraps because eggs at a level threepence paid well. The ordinary restrictions on the production and sale of eggs were unworkable in a number of isolated areas, including Wester Ross. There was plenty of demand for eggs within the uncontrolled area, and we all sold them at the recognised wholesale price. Outside the area we could legally charge only the retail price, which, by one of the curiosities of war-time economics, was less than the wholesale. (Of the subsidies paid to keep down the cost of living, some, including those on eggs and potatoes, were paid at the wholesale level.) Strangers in flashy suits called at the house offering much higher prices. In Campbeltown the price rose above 9d. per egg. We had no proof that these men were collecting for the black market, but if the organisers of the black market did not try to tap the uncontrolled areas they did not know their job. That is a charge I have not heard levelled at them.

We were able to buy some Exchequer hens locally—elegant black and white birds, each feather wholly white or wholly black. We set Rhode Island eggs under a broody, and bought in some day-old Rhode Island pullets. There had recently been difficulty over these, I remember : one of the stranger consequences of the Pearl Harbour attack was that male chicks could masquerade as females, the Japanese experts who did the sexing having been interned. We built up a flock of Rhode Islands as soon as we had the corn and the chats (unsellable) to feed them. The breed does well in the district. Our birds averaged something over 200 eggs a year and made reasonable carcases. We always kept a few dual-purpose ducks also —Khaki Campbells. The ducks and above all the ducklings were a joy to have around the steading, and so too were the young chicks ; but the only thing I really liked about the hens was the price of eggs. There is, I do not doubt, a fascination in serious work with hens—in building up a first-rate flock, trap-nesting, systematic culling, and refinements like progeny-testing ; and as an embodiment of abounding health nothing could surpass the brilliant scarlet and white of Donald's Leghorns on a summer day. But hens in themselves are brainless and slightly sordid creatures. Their whole emotional range seems to run only from indignation to consternation. They stand miserably in exposed places when it is raining, seek out flapping objects for the joy of being frightened, and cackle interminably and insufferably. There can be no species in which the note of alarm is harder to distinguish from that of achievement. A kind of chain-reaction always threatens : if enough of them are present, a single cackle can set off the whole lot, and one small egg, or the false rumour of an egg, can make the Sabbath hideous. They are perverse. You provide clean, dry, comfortable, secluded hay nests for them to lay in, and they spurn it in favour of some rain-swept clump of rashes. They are obstinate. If they once pick on some corner of the barn or byre for a nest, they besiege the building for hours, hopping from one foot to the other, until at last a chink is left open in door or window, when they scurry in to deposit the waiting egg. And they are stupid, stupid beyond words. With my own eyes I have seen a hen lay her egg on top of a pile of grain, walk two yards, and start scratching anxiously for food.

Ducks, on the other hand, are intelligent, brave, exuberant and irresistibly funny. Much of their food they find for themselves, converting slugs into eggs ; they do not peck aimlessly around, but work in formation across the field. Even at feeding time they waddle between food and water while the hens are consuming the food. They accept the good weather and revel in the bad. Some ducklings of ours hatched out at the beginning of a dry spell and were quite large before their first rain fell. It converted the Wee Park near the house into a pond and they were delirious. Nothing I could do would drive them in that night. Ducks do not stand around looking aggrieved when food is late, but quack peremptorily in chorus. They seem to while away the early morning until they are let out by dribbling the eggs up and down, making them filthy though never breaking them ; and as a mark of intelligence the bursts of raucous applause that mark the finer points do at any rate invite comparison with the cheer-leading at college games. For as long as they lay at all, ducks lay every morning. But they too have their weak points. Their eggs are less in demand than hen eggs. They too are inclined to lay in remote corners, especially when broody. They will then come in at meal times, leaving their nests carefully camouflaged, and will make a devious return with a wary eye for observers. We seldom found the nests except by accident. Once or twice a duck came in from the Lower Flat with an unauthorised brood of squeaking ducklings. They are poor mothers. The ducklings get trodden on, left at the foot of banks, or swept away on streams, until there are no more to vanish. The ducks themselves are apt to vanish where there are foxes and other nocturnal dangers. But the chief merit of ducks, as creatures that will be much under your eyes all the year round, and economic considerations apart, is the variety of their comic attitudes, from the sleeping party (all heads tucked round on the sunny side, and one eye open for danger), to the foraging party (all heads down and all tails up but waggling).

Slang usage bears me out; the duck has given us a term of affection and the hen a term of abuse. An "old duck" and an "old hen" are two very different things.

For a while we had trouble with the hens. For week after week, until there could be little question of coincidence, we had fewer eggs on Sundays than on weekdays. Even in the Highlands this seemed odd. Then we noticed that eggs left on the grass for a few minutes might vanish completely. We ruled out rats, dogs and hoodies. A half-eaten egg gave us the clue. The hens were let out rather later on Sundays and if there were egg-eaters amongst them they would be subjected then to more prolonged temptation. As a test we left some eggs in the shut henhouse overnight, and by morning seven had gone.

It is an awkward habit. One hen finds a broken egg, or perhaps pecks at the shell of an egg when she needs lime, and gets the taste of the contents. She suddenly learns that she has nothing to lose but her chains. She teaches others. Soon a revolutionary situation threatens. The only certain cure for an egg-eater is to put her in

the pot, but that is costly : she is worth much more as
a going concern. We tried the common recipe first—
eggshells stuffed with an unthinkable mixture of mustard
and crude paraffin. Some were wholly consumed and
still the trouble continued. We tried decoy eggs, and
I took to peering through chinks and making surprise
raids. With much loss of time we identified the three or
four birds responsible and put them in a run away from
the others. Here they could at most eat only their own
eggs, but they did not eat any at all. After a few weeks
of segregation with mustard eggs as a reminder, they
appeared to be cured. Meanwhile the egg yield had risen,
on Sundays and weekdays alike, until it came close to
the limit of one egg per hen per day. We did know a
lady who was getting thirteen eggs from twelve hens and
a cock. She never discovered whether the extra egg should
be placed to the discredit of the cock or to the credit of
a Stakhanovite hen.

Strict chronology would require that all this should
wait till a later chapter. I have only reached the harvest
that enabled us to start taking the poultry more seriously.
Our few poultry had themselves made the harvest more
difficult. They had discovered the corn as it ripened, for
they had of course free range, and had flattened some
parts of the field. The ducks with their broad build and
waddling gait did more harm than the hens. For as long
as possible we kept them penned, but they moped and
the number of eggs dwindled. On the Island the crofters
had solved this problem by moving the hens completely
to turf and stone huts on the machair, far removed from
all corn during the summer. There it was a more serious
matter, because adjacent strips had different owners. It
is not easy to love your neighbour when his hens are in
your corn.

The same broken weather that had hampered the hay
and corn harvest delayed our start upon the potatoes.
Unlike corn and hay most varieties of potatoes can wait
without deteriorating ; but the days grow shorter and

colder and there is the ultimate threat of frost. Several times I asked Donald's advice, but his reply was : " Hopeless. They'd float off down the drills." So we got on with other work and waited.

When at last a start seemed possible, it was on a market day when Donald had taken stirks to Dingwall. I had never tried ploughing at all, and a drill-plough has more tricks even than an ordinary plough. Besides darting to left and right, and rolling, it can dive so deep that the horses are halted by the sudden weight of earth and shoot up again so that they leap forward with nothing at all to pull. It can also, if the point catches one of the hidden stones that abound, pivot abruptly into the air and break a man's neck. Several neighbours, however, had come to see if we would be starting, and we resolved to try. Mrs. Ferguson led the horses while I took the handles. At the first drill the plough followed a course that would not be surprising in a fish, bird or aeroplane, but which was very odd on a potato field. Tubers and half-tubers were scattered around, more were still buried. The second drill was hardly less erratic, but the third improved. We did manage to lift and cart a certain number before nightfall.

Next day was another matter. Donald was at the handles. The plough behaved very differently—and so did the horses. Donald ploughed out alternate drills, and then we worked along with our pails, usually one person to a drill. I will not pretend that it is holiday work. For back-ache it is worse than corn-lifting, the earth is cold and wet and scratchy to the hands, and often much rummaging and poking are needed to expose the tubers. Nobody ever grumbled—and nobody was there under compulsion. We worked in line, again, so that conversation and back-chat were possible. They greatly speeded the work, and so also did the slight element of personal rivalry. In so far as there was rivalry each of us, I suppose, was not truly working at his own chosen speed ; but at least the stimulus is very different from

that of the potato-spinner, which has just the same effect
as our experiment with the mower on corn : it spaces
out the workers and, if the farmer orders the spacing
wisely, induces a panic-stricken haste to clear the way
for the on-coming monster. Moreover, as the co-operation was voluntary, we could straighten our backs without
needing to be furtive. That is the worst thing in being
a paid man, the feeling that you've sold your time (the
most precious of all commodities) for 1s. 6d. an hour,
and must keep to the bargain. No, not quite the worst :
the worst is the outlook of the apprentice who, on being
shown how to cut extra soles from a piece of leather,
remarked : " Not —— likely. That would be saving
money for the boss."

The potatoes that were dry enough we made into a
rough clamp (or " grave " or " pit ") covering them
temporarily with rashes only, so that air would circulate.
The others we carted to a shed.

Next morning there was heavy rain. Days and weeks
went by and not a potato could we lift. The rain washed
over the rock by the house and in at the back door until
we had to wear gum-boots in the scullery. Worse still,
snow appeared on the hill-tops, and came closer and
closer. We straightened up the clamp and earthed it
over for safety. Snow and frost came ; by good luck
snow came first. A warm white coat lay between the
drills and the frost. Potatoes will stand four degrees of
frost without harm. When at last our chance came we
were within a month of the shortest day.

Half of our potatoes—those from the alternate drills
—were safe, but none of Donald's ; we arranged there-
for to tackle his first. Here and there a drill had already
been lifted with the graip (or dung-fork) : by the neighbours who had a drill or two in the field, or by Lizzie
for the house. We kept a tally of the drills finished, and
argued whether three, four or five days would see us
through. By now the tups were on the hill, and towards
dusk I would slip away with the dog to bunch the ewes

with the tups. From the top I could see the activity on
the field : the rows of backs, the big cart wheeling in the
day's achievement, and the children helping or playing.
Disconsolate cows waited for the comfort of the byre.
" Hoick, Dick, Hoick," I could hear, and sometimes the
clear shouts of the children. On the last afternoon one
of the tups was missing. Before I had found him it was
dark and the work below had been finished. I joined the
crowd at supper, where everyone was in rare good humour.
A perennial argument, half-serious and half-jocular, was
already in progress. The married folk were extolling
matrimony, and the younger folk the blessedness of the
single state. Donald, a bachelor, but by no means a confirmed bachelor, pointed out that no one there had a good
word for marriage but the married, who must keep up a
show, if only to save face. Mrs. McL. retorted that only
the married had studied both sides of the matter. We
were in no hurry and lingered by the fire talking of the
year's crops, and the expected dance at Balmacara, and
much else that I now forget.

On the kitchen wall hung a framed rhyme-sheet that
had been sent by Mrs. McK. to Donald to plague him,
when she was away on holiday. It ran something like
this. (I quote from memory, and can only apologise to
the owner of the copyright, whoever he may be.)

A REGULAR GIRL

I want a girl who is good and is pretty,
But not so blamed good that she cannot be witty.
I want a girl who is saving and thrifty,
But not so blamed mean that she cannot dress nifty.
I want a girl who can talk well, of course,
But not one who talks till she talks herself hoarse.
I don't want a pippin, a peach or a pearl,
In fact what I want is a regular girl.

To this insult injury was added by a neighbour who

mounted the following retort upon a map of the Hydro-Electric development project for the district :

A WISE AULD WIFE

" Conceit o' the men," the auld wifie exclaimed,
When she saw my requirements printed and framed.
" She maun deck hersel' oot, yet nae spend sae muckle
But the crock in the corner shall hae a wee puckle.
She'll abominate gossip yet love a right chat ;
She maunna be this an' she's boun' to do that.
Sic rubies as yon mayna come when ye ca' :
If ye dinna watch oot ye'll hae nae lass at a' ! "

And now, with the season's crops all safely garnered in, we could face the winter's work and the winter's relaxation.

Splitting potato drills. Miss Stewart's croft was wholly encircled by Achbeg ground.

Rolled ground. Dottacks Park seen from The Face. Field work often makes interesting patterns.

Cattle in winter. They are waiting to be let into the byre.

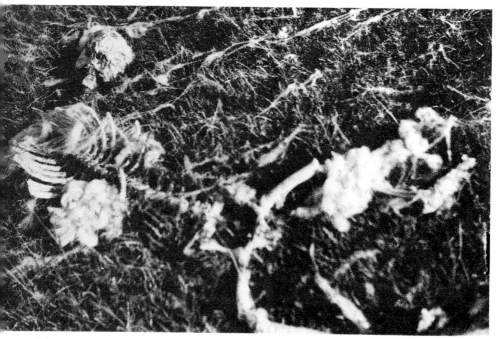

A lost sheep. The buzzards take over from the maggots.

CHAPTER VII

SHEEP—WINTER

" Be thou diligent to know the state of thy flocks and look well
to thy herds."—" Proverbs."

It is because the end of the winter marks the natural
break in the year's work that crofts usually change hands
at the May Term; but the culmination of the work, and
especially of the sheep work, is the autumn sales.

Scottish sales are better managed than English. Behind
the covered sale-ring itself lies a vast orderly jungle of
pens and alleys. Batches of beasts are everywhere, pushing
at gates, poking through barriers, racing along the alleys,
nuzzling, prodding, charging. Yardsmen shout and
whistle; little boys whack; pigs cry murder; calves
bawl themselves hoarse for their mothers and cows for
their calves. On some market-days the noise seemed to
envelop the whole of Dingwall, like an audible fog. In
all this pandemonium and seeming chaos there are, say,
a handful of Achbeg lambs, or a couple of weaned calves.
They will in due course find their way into the ring, where
they will fall to the highest bidder; they will return to
their pen; the buyer will receive the right beasts and
I shall receive the right cheque. During the day many
thousand head of stock will change hands. Unimaginable
confusion could arise; but somehow it doesn't. An
occasional small lamb will wriggle through the bars, and
there is, of course, plenty of scope for deliberate error,
but mishaps are remarkably rare. In the office enormous
sums of money are being scribbled at reckless speed on
to cheque forms; crowds of frightened beasts find their
way into lorries and railway-trucks; and by nightfall the
whole bewildering transaction will be straightened out.

The pivot of all this organisation is the ring itself,

where the auctioneer, a man of rare bodily and mental gifts, out-bawls the tremendous hubbub. You may imagine him in his high rostrum, note-book in hand, peering from a region of tobacco-smoke at this human and animal throng with the eyes of Argus himself.

"There's a fine bull-calf, now, gentlemen.—What is it, Tom?—Yes, a bull-calf, gentlemen. Did you see a better this morning? Who'll say seven pounds to get us started? Seven pounds? Six pounds? Just *look* at him, gentlemen, worth ten guineas if he's worth a penny. Will nobody start me off at six pounds for this bonny bull-calf? —Gentleman over there says five pounds; right then. Five pounds—five ten—six—six ten—seven—seven ten— why couldn't we save time and *start* at that?—a fine blocky calf, gentlemen—seven ten—seven twelve—fourteen—six- teen—eighteen—eight—two—four—six—guineas—ten— twelve—fourteen—fourteen—any advance on fourteen— eight fourteen—going at eight fourteen—sixteen—eighteen —nine—two—nine two—nine two—going at nine two— no advance on nine two—now's your chance, sir—no advance on nine two?—nine four?—right then (smack goes the note-book)—sold at nine two to Mr. MacH., Ardbean."

The vocal powers of the salesmen are hardly more remarkable than their memory. Whilst rattling off prices and exhortations at immense speed they have still attention left over to recall details of lots long after they have passed through the ring, and they even notice, in mid-career, clerical slips in the numbering.

The yardsmen too take a pride in their accuracy, and especially in the rapidity with which they count lots. A broad gate is thrown open and sheep pour into the ring, four or five abreast, leaping like dolphins. "Ninety-three," calls the head yardsman, and ninety-three it almost cer- tainly will be. Local wit says that they count the hoofs and divide by four.

In the ring there is an air of tense drama—or rather of tense sport, for nobody can foresee the next act. At any moment the course of events may take a new twist. But it is a limited kind of drama, or sport. " We needs must love the highest when we see it "—certainly, the highest price.

Money is being made in the ring, but so too are reputations. Here, nothing succeeds like success. Keen bidding on a beast may reflect not only the good appearance of the beast itself but also the general esteem of the seller. For even the best judge of sheep cannot be sure how a batch will thrive on his ground if he does not know, by repute at least, the ground and the flock they come from. Especially is this true with tups. Two tups may look alike and behave alike in every detail, yet one, having been primed for sale with hand-feeding, will immediately sicken when put out on to the coarse heather and grass, while the other will settle at once to his work. The only safeguard is familiarity with the reputation of the breeder. Farmers, particularly sheep farmers, therefore take great pains to build up a reputation.

Part of the tenseness of the ring is due neither to the sporting nor to the dramatic interest then, but to the knowledge that here farmers are being weighed in the balance : it is the tenseness of the examination-room. In a rough way the buyers are delivering judgment on the sellers. A Chinese peasant sells little. He feeds and clothes his family largely off his own ground, and he hopes to pass on as good a farm as he inherited. The years alone can judge his skill. In a lesser degree crofters are in that position, too, but on the whole farming, including crofting, is now farming for sale, and the verdict lies with the account-books. To convert five-pounds-worth of calf-food into four-pounds-worth of veal may be a pleasant hobby, but it is not farming—only a minority, in the nature of things, can make a loss. However, the justice of the ring is a very rough justice. Prices at 11 a.m. may fall heavily for no better reason than that word has reached the dealers that there's whisky in at " The Caledonian." There are many extraneous influences that raise or depress prices, from the weather (which may have kept most of the potential bidders busy at their harvesting) to rumours of the raising of the ban on Irish cattle. Neither does the ring take account of land-racking. Some at least of the farmers who were driven to bankruptcy or suicide between the two wars were honest, able men who refused to farm by methods unacceptable to their consciences.

Occasional markets are held in outlying parts, either in a rough fank or perhaps in a field by a lochside. In the Outer Isles the sale days are treated as holidays. Everybody who can leave his croft goes to the sale, whether or not he has business to transact. At one that I saw, in the middle of all the jostling clamour, occurred an incident that I remember vividly. An old man had bought a young cow and the cow knew her own mind. She set off downhill for home at an impressive speed. But the man also knew his mind. Not liking the thought of walking the length of the Island to fetch the cow again, he hung on rigidly to the halter and on knees, elbows and probably chin he tobogganed down the hill and out of sight. He was in his holiday clothes. A special danger attaches to the homing instinct of these cattle at some markets. They may have been driven to market at low tide across fords from the smaller islands. If they break away after the sale, they may make for home, attempt to swim across the unexpected water, and in all likelihood be swept off to sea by the tidal current. The inns prosper on market day. Buyers and sellers who have done well celebrate their gain, and the others drown their misfortunes. I saw an ordinary crofter lay down three pound notes, the price of a couple of cast ewes, and put the change in the hospital box. Dealers who travel with the salesmen compete with local buyers, and on the whole prices seemed fair. One sometimes heard of islands where a dealer abused a position of monopoly, but there are too many dealers looking for "a good thing" and the crofters are too well informed about prices and values for such instances to be common.

Most beasts, however, went to Dingwall or Inverness, and a long day the sale-day was for us in the West. The morning train left Stromeferry at 6.30. Cattle and sheep must be driven to the station before this, with a certain margin for trucking and a wide margin for the odd beast that must leap a fence or make off along the line. There might also be jobs to be done around the steading before departure, and again when we arrived home at night. We in the Glen were within two miles of the station : many crofts had ten times that distance of road travel in addition to the rail journey, and some considerably more. The main disadvantage to the West was not time lost but rather the dead weight of fares and freight. The seller in the ring has the option of withdrawing if the highest bid does not please him, but a seller from the West, unable to afford the triple freight, knows that he must take what is offered ; and the buyers also know. There is no suggestion of trickery here ; it is simply that the ardour of the bidders is damped down. Bidding is on the whole keenest in the middle of the day. At first, bids are slow and erratic, until buyers have got the feeling of the day's market : they tend to play safe. One sale started with a burst of optimism after which prices fell, and the best sale of the day was the first. That is very rare. Prices tail off at the end of the day also : buyers, having quenched their thirst for a bargain, turn aside to quench a more elementary thirst. It is said that the order of places on the catalogue is established by lot, but small farmers from the West felt, rightly or wrongly, that chance too often gave them the bad positions. One of them, normally an outstandingly quiet-living man, was stirred to angry remonstrance of a very positive kind. Chance took the hint.

There were, fortunately, two independent rings in Dingwall (they referred to each other as The Opposition), and we could go on to Inverness at only slightly added cost.

Our first sale was to be the lamb sale towards the end

of August. We had a bad day for the gathering, with steady rain and gusts of wind. The sheep tried every trick they knew to avoid coming out of the shelter of Strome Wood, doubling back, scattering, climbing out on to ledges, and defying the dogs. Donald and I were soon drenched : no clothing will keep you dry when you are scrambling up and down precipitous slopes deep in bracken, and war-time boots were never waterproof for long. By two o'clock we had most of them in the steading, and separated out the wedder lambs for market. Donald was selling all his lambs, his being a flying stock. A number of sheep that needed attention for maggot kept us busy till evening, and then we put the ewes in a remote well-fenced park up the Glen. Those that had had their lambs taken from them kept up a pitiful bleating. Finally we herded the lambs up to the railway pens on the brow of the hill above Strome, and stood in the rain until darkness had fallen and the lambs had quietened down. They would lie under banks and clumps of rashes until morning, although they knew the ground well and the weak points in the fences. The ewes when we came down to the Glen again were still bleating through the darkness and the rain. Some by now were probably through the first fences. They would filter back towards the steading where their lambs had been taken from them, but they would be very unlikely to find their lambs before morning.

At 3.45 next morning we were making ready. The lambs were trucked in the early morning light. We shared trucks with some other men who were going to the same market. As usual, the morning train was pretty quiet. At Dingwall, after breakfast at a cafe, we helped the yardsmen who were taking batches of lambs along to the sale-yards from the station. Towns are full of objects that are frightening to a lamb, and especially dogs. From Pekes to Great Danes they loiter on the pavements, most of them wholly indifferent to the sheep, but none the less the source of terror to a lamb that has never before been

away from its mother and has now been subjected to the
clanging and buffeting of seventy miles in a cattle-truck.
At a crossroad a few did break away and were only re-
trieved after a vigorous quarter of an hour of hare-and-
hounds. I was glad they all had their distinctive keelmarks.
When cattle and sheep are driven through busy shopping
streets, queer things will happen. Ewes watch for open
shop-doors and it may have been on some such occasion that the proverbial bull in a china shop earned this
reputation. The nearest story to that that I actually heard
concerned a bull that entered a front door in Plockton,
walked up the stairs, and surveyed the world from the
window, with a curtain draped on either horn. A looker-on
was able to record the incident with his camera.

The mixed batch of lambs were separated at the shedder
in the yard and taken to their respective pens. Friends
with a reputation as sheep men were invited to comment
on the " drawing," which is an important matter. If a
farmer has two hundred lambs to put through the ring,
he will not send them all in together. Some of them will
be poorer than others—smaller, badly built, swine-mouthed
or otherwise defective. Buyers will tend to bid on the
poorer lambs since they will have to pay one price for
them all. Hence he will " draw out " the poorest lambs,
or " shots," to be sold separately, and probably divide
the others also into classes. The shepherd, who usually
knows far more about sheep than his master and whose
word normally prevails when there are differences of judgment, cannot be wholly trusted here. His interest is to
" top the ring "—to get the highest price, whether on a
few lambs or many. The owner has naturally the same
wish. The price of his " tops " will be quoted in the
paper and discussed all over the West for long to come.
Not merely his pride is involved, but his business reputation, which (as we have said) is a business asset. But
the owner has a second interest not necessarily shared
equally by the shepherd, that of getting the highest total
sum from the sale. I well remember the chagrin of a certain

crofter. Not liking the top bid on his sheep he took them out of the ring unsold, and later in the day put them through the ring in two batches. He obtained a better figure on his " tops "—but later found, on calculating it out, that he would have done better to have taken the first offer.

In the ring I felt very much out of place at first, " shooing " the lambs around and trying to follow the bidding. The salesman's rigmarole doubtless looks straightforward enough as I have transcribed it earlier, but the words are very hard to pick out in the universal noise, and everything occurs at top speed. Moreover, the bidding is very puzzling to the beginner. There is a convention that you must hide all signs of keenness about any beasts you are interested in, for fear that a rival bidder or a friend of the seller will chase you higher than you need have risen. Accordingly the buyers have some agreed signal known to the salesman. The merest flick of a cigarette or hunching of shoulders, given off-handedly without any pause in a ringside conversation, and without so much as a glance at the salesman, means, " Yes, I'll pay that." However closely you watch it is usually hard to know who is bidding, and it can happen that two friends standing side by side may unknowingly bid against each other and both suppose they have bought the lot. However, I was quite pleased with the sale. We were far from topping the ring—Achbeg hill will never carry sheep that can do that—but prices were a shilling up on last year, and reasonable enough.

Our business done we went out into the town to shop, and to celebrate. The return train in the evening is naturally less quiet. There was on this occasion animated talk about the day's prices, and there were songs—not " Roll out the Barrel," but " Fiunary " and " Caisteal a Ghlinne " and many more. At Achnasheen there is usually a wait, for the two trains from east and from west cross here. As soon as our train drew up men jumped off and hurried over the bridge to the inn, in search of one more quick drink before they returned to their lonely glens. A shepherd who was travelling with us returned crestfallen. " No drink," he said, " there isn't a drop." " Not even beer ? " I asked. " Oh, yes, there's beer."

Strome Brae seemed very steep that night, but, as we all came over the boggy flat, several lights were gleaming pleasantly in the Glen, blackout or no.

Half the ewes were now rid of their lambs, and as soon as they had recovered from the pangs of separation they settled down to making the most of what remained of the summer grazing. There was no such holiday yet for the mothers of the ewe lambs. However, it was necessary to get the ewe lambs away to wintering soon, and three weeks later Donald and I were gathering in the rain and separating and keeling the lambs once more. Ours were to go to wintering with Tom's, who had, of course, far more than our little bunch. At about five Tom came up the road from Achmore bridge with his lambs before him, and ours joined the larger flock. They gave little trouble, though lambs can be very lively ; a few keep bounding away from the edge of the flock, to be frightened back by the watchful dogs. We put them into one of the pens, twined branches in weak parts of the wire, and talked till all was quiet. Tom told me many stories of more prosperous sheep-farming days.

Hours before train-time next morning there came a thunderous knocking at the door and Tom's voice calling, " Are you awake there, Mr. O'Malley, boy ? " Tom lived for his sheep and left nothing to chance. I saw several pipes glowing in the darkness, those of neighbours who had come to help with the trucking. We trooped up to the pens, where all was quiet. For an hour or so yet there could be no light for driving the lambs down to Strome. We therefore found a hollow bank and lay listening to the wind in the heather just above our heads. From beyond Loch Carron, hidden in blackness, a light or two flashed across, sign that others had business with the early train.

The men talked, usually (at my request) in Gaelic, and the sudden flare of a match sometimes picked out a face and some dead heather. Very gradually the profile of Gladstone's Face showed against the lighter sky, and the loch below picked up the gathering brightness. Just as soon as we could discern one another, Tom announced, " Well, boys, we'll be moving."

Stepping carefully amongst the boggy places two men went round the lambs and at the gate we counted them. All were there. They were keen to make uphill towards home and their mothers, not downhill towards the unknown, but we trucked them without incident, checked and double-checked the door-fastenings, and saw them off for the winter. They went in three trucks but would come back later in at least four; the Kyle ferry charges 1d. a hogg on the outward journey but 1½d. on the return. That is the measure of the importance of the first winter.

All the lambs should now have been off the ground, but things never work so precisely in hill-farming. One or two had been kept back as they were not yet clear of maggot and others came out of the wood at their leisure. Some of these we sold locally. Two of them went to Isabella, who would keep them in a barn, feed them on hay and small potatoes, and make good sheep of them by spring. The others I tried to keep in the parks over the winter, but only one survived. Within a few days one of them had fallen on its side and the hoodies pecked out its eyes.

Early in October we " gathered " yet again for the cast ewe sale. Once more we had a bad day for gathering, wet and extremely windy. Up on the Face there was a wind you could lean hard against and I saw Prince in the Middle Park below edging backwards and sideways and diagonally and all ways in an effort to graze yet keep his tail into the wind. The sale went off much as the lamb sale had done. Cold sunshine flooded the Dingwall streets and we thought of the good day we were losing with corn and potatoes still out. But back at home it was raining, as we learned that evening. Owing to the formation of the mountains, there is rarely good weather on both sides of the Highlands at once. The west wind brings rain to the west, the east to the east—and the west wind prevails. We took it for granted that the rain would begin at Achnasheen on our return journey, and were seldom wrong.

There were other early starts for the morning train, mostly to do with cattle. Several of our neighbours were sending off weaned calves (six-month-old sucker calves) and I helped with the trucking. The easiest way to take the calves down was to let them follow their mothers; then it was my job to drive the mothers home as I was not going on the train. The cows were black and the morning was also black. My torch revealed nothing at all but a white " sock " on one of the cows. I drove them somehow into a park and came back at dawn to count them. All were there, but they soon broke out and made for the station in search of their calves. For days and nights afterwards the Glen was full of desolate mooings. Another morning there were older cattle to be trucked. I think that was the occasion when some Highlanders also were to go. Dazzling candles and flash-lamps at the pens caught the eyes and the enormous horns of the cattle. Much scuffling could be heard, panting, oaths, loud shouts; eventually a triumphant slam and the brushing of market clothes. Orion sprawled overhead, but he helped not at all.

Lastly there was the tup sale—the only sale at which I was a buyer. We had taken over two tups at the valuation, but one had died miserably : half-eaten by maggot he had leaped from a rock and dislocated his spine. Of all the sides of sheep-work requiring judgment none is so critical as the choice of a tup. Luckily I had friends to advise me, and picked up a good enough young tup fairly cheap.

The two tups were put together in one of the parks, where they sparred a little before settling down amicably. The intention was that they should remain in the park (we had chosen that with the best walls) and that the ewes should remain out of the park, until about 27th November.

The sheep, however, had no use for the social decencies. Fully a month earlier the ewes, when they had an interest in the tups, came round on to the Face above the park and bleated noisily and (no doubt) seductively. From then on no Achbeg fence or dyke would hold them. Donald's tup was giving similar trouble, and in sun, rain and snow, morning and evening, on weekdays and Sundays alike, when the alarm was sounded, we had to drop all other work for a rough cross-country chase. The only chance was to bring them in with a bunch of ewes. A single tup will not usually run from a dog but will stand and box it, or run at it; indeed one can sometimes " drive " a tup short distances by keeping the dog on the *wrong* side of him. A neighbour offered us the use of a small park with high netting fences in addition to hedges, and thereafter we had less trouble.

By law, no tups may be on the hill outside a fixed period. Early lambs are quite likely to die from hunger and expo- sure and the mother, even if she pulls the lamb through, will do so at heavy cost to herself. Further, tups may wander for miles and become a danger to all the flocks in the district. Shepherds take a pride in having no prema- ture lambs in their flock, and a lapse means leg-pulling. Our errant tups were responsible for a few early lambs in Tom's flock next spring.

" Well, Tom," I said when I met him one morning later on, not knowing how he would take it, " I see you've lambs already. These things will happen in the best- regulated flocks." But the grass was coming on well and Tom was in a smiling humour.

" Yes, Mr. O'Malley, boy," he retorted, " I've more lambs on the place than some people will have when the lambing's over and done with."

During these tup-hunts I was fortunate in having a new collie, Nell. Major had been needed by John after

all and I had answered many advertisements before getting
Nell. She was growing too old for regular sheep work on
high ground, but would manage some years of less strenuous work yet. The first time I took her on the hill, to
drive ewes farther from the parks, there was a desperate
muddle. Nell, it seemed, had been trained to other signals,
probably whistles. When I gave a signal, therefore, anything might happen ; when I tried to countermand the
signal there was no foreseeing the further consequences.
By the time we came off the hill I was in a furious temper
and convinced that my pig-in-a-poke deal had been a
fiasco. In a few days, however, we had learned to understand each other and from then onwards she was a joy to
work. She lived for her work. If she saw me move towards
the door she would be at my heels ; if I took down a stick,
she was overjoyed, and if I reached for the binoculars
hardly anything would hold her. Whenever we came
within sight of a sheep she would crouch and glance over
her shoulder pleading for permission to fetch it ; in conversation I had to be careful to make no gesture that Nell
could turn to her own ends. At first she felt underworked,
having less to do here than with the shepherd who had
sold her. She slipped off from the potato-field unnoticed.

" Why, look at Nell," said Mrs. MacB., after a while,
" she's tidied up all the sheep in the park. That's the way
she thinks sheep ought to be."

The sheep were not mine. I had to be severe with
her, not merely because the owner might object, but
because a dog that works without orders will soon be
blamed, however wrongly, for any sheep-worrying that
may occur. She soon settled down to a quieter life.

The intelligence of a sheep-dog is almost uncanny. She
knows the ways of sheep, she knows the ground, and she
knows the wishes of humans. It is best, of course, to keep
inflexibly to a particular set of signals with any dog : she
cannot really understand adverbs and comparatives and
such-like. Yet so intelligent is her behaviour that one
almost inevitably slips into spoken instructions like :

" No, not that way—wider up, Nell, wider up," which must lead to some degree of confusion in her mind.

Donald trained a young dog who was less biddable than Nell close in, but who became excellent at working wide out. Just as far as voice could carry or gesture be seen he would bunch the sheep for Donald, beat around for more and bring them all in. Our two dogs then made a good pair. Like most sheep-dogs they would work for one master only.

Nell had been trained to fetch cattle also, and I taught her to bring in the ducks at night. At first she was completely oblivious of the ducks. When I sent her out to where they were rummaging for slugs, she rushed around searching for sheep, yelping with frustration, and scattering the ducks without so much as seeing them. About the third or fourth time I made the attempt, she very suddenly saw the point. The moment of realisation was just as definite as that at which a child sees the point of a question. She immediately started zig-zagging, " wearing " them in towards me as though they were sheep. From then onwards she put them in at night. Hens and chicks she ignored completely ; and yet when later on there was a hen with ducklings she at once showed interest. For hours she headed them away from what she conceived to be danger, to the great indignation of the hen, to whom the greatest of all dangers was an interfering dog.

A little while before the tups go out to the hill, the sheep are given their second compulsory dip of the year. This time a boiler is kept going beside the fank, partly because the dip employed needs hot water, partly out of consideration for the sheep. We had bad weather for the job. After the sheep had been gathered they were kept waiting in the parks for several days while sleet made dipping impossible. At length, when the weather seemed a little better, we dipped the Fernaig ewes but drenching rain came down before evening. Very little dip can there have been in the fleeces after a night of such rain. Our ewes were put through the bath next day, and in similar weather. We could now sign our dipping papers ; that was something at least achieved.

We were still at the potatoes (as has been said) when on 27th November the tups at last were put to the hill. Now it was the gimmers that must be kept in, except for the few who were let out after a fortnight. (If they are to lamb it is better for them to lamb late.) Every day I ought to have gone to the hill, checked the whereabouts of the tups, and rounded the ewes in to them, but it was a time-taking job ; to be really thorough in Strome Wood would require the whole of every day, and more. Fortunately this is a matter in which Nature is a willing helper.

When the tups came in from the hill, six or seven weeks later, one of them (having served his two years) was due to be marketed. If he remained longer in the flock he would be mating with his own progeny, with the danger of the pairing of awkward recessives that then arises. He fetched only his mutton value, a seventh of the price John had paid two years previously ; yet he was still young enough and sound. When possible, exchanges are made, and save a good deal of money, provided the animal survives. Tups are strangely delicate for all their manly seeming.

On the first day of April the hoggs returned, bounding with energy, and making the other sheep seem old and tired by contrast—as indeed they were. After ear-marking them we put them in the parks for a few days to settle. One of the great enemies of the sheep, and especially of the hoggs, is a plant that abounds in Scotland, though it is the symbol of England, the briar-rose. We had many by the banks and in corners of the fields. There is no plant, even the rowan, that has such breath-taking beauty at all seasons, but they are a plague to sheep. Their thorns waste much wool, and they are the death of many. Hoggs are particularly apt to fall a prey to them as their coats are so thick and they have still to learn much that a canny old ewe knows in her bones. Once they are caught, their struggles only ensnare them further. Unless the shepherd finds them in time, exposure, starvation or shock will finish what the briars have begun. A hogg that I was keeping in the Road Park became entangled three times, and the third time she was almost lost. For a couple of days I did not visit the park. On the third day I missed her and found her hopelessly enmeshed and nearly worn out. Her struggles had made bare a complete circle in the grass. When I let her loose, having keeled her un-willingly from my pricked fingers, she staggered towards the nearest ewe. Though twelve months old and six months off her mother, she tried to feed from the ewe, who gently repulsed her. It must have been a reversion to childish ways under the stress of hunger and fear. I cut down many briars in the parks but there were always more. They were at all times a menace to the sheep in the woods, where bones around a bush may mark the scene of a struggle that occurred perhaps last year, perhaps many years ago—who can tell?

A high-pitched piping drew attention to twin lambs up on a ledge, three weeks before their time. I carried them down inside my jacket to a safer place, with the mother following close at heel. Though everything was against her she made a good job of the two lambs before autumn. Ordinarily twins are separated, one being given to a ewe who has lost her lamb. She does not usually take willingly to the change. The shepherd puts her in a small enclosure with the changeling, which has tied upon it the skin of the dead lamb. Smelling her own lamb the ewe is the more likely to accept the newcomer. With a small flock, however, and with the difficulty of making a morning and evening round every day (as the good shepherd does) when spring work on the arable is at greatest pressure, a crofter cannot always make the exchange. Whenever possible I went up to the hill during the lambing weeks; but I soon found that the ewes bore their lambs very competently without me, whereas the fields left to themselves bore nothing but weeds. Where a choice had to be made, therefore, I chose to work on

Haystacks. Beyond them, the Lower Flat and The Face.

Prince rolling. His first reaction to being turned loose.

Birch tree twisted by wind.   View across the Glen to Meallan.

"The Mill."   Burnt-out space in Strome Wood; it was here that we bunched the sheep to force them out of the wood.

the arable. Any help I could have given at the actual lambing would have a very doubtful value, and I resolved only to intervene in the last resource. There was, so far as I was aware, only one occasion in the three years' lambing when my help might have saved a ewe. A report reached me that a ewe had been seen from the ferry to be having trouble, but we arrived too late. The lamb had mispresented. It was a terrible crimson in the face and the mother too had died from exhaustion. We did, of course, lose lambs that better shepherding would have saved ; but we were at least spared a trouble that had brought losses to Willy McG., who had been tenant before John. In his day many of the ewes had chosen to lamb beside the river, so close to the bank that the lamb was no sooner born than drowned. It is startling that instinctive behaviour, which can look so much like intelligence, can yet jump the rails so completely. A bulling cow will leap at an old coat on the line, a skylark will nest where its young will surely be trampled, and a moth will singe itself to death on the lamp chimney.

Throughout the spring we received warnings and exhortations vilely mimeographed from the landlords, to be careful about heather-burning. In their own interest the Forestry authorities send their men to help at the more critical parts of the burning. We were at the bottom of the list ; there were so few good days for burning that our turn never came in the first spring. For several weeks, despite the unfavourable weather, the sky was overcast with an ominous grey-brown cloud, and everywhere was the scent of burning. At night we saw distant fires twinkling on the smaller islands, on Applecross, and on Skye.

Burning can be intoxicating work. Under the influence of the height, the breeze, the spurts of furious beating, and the primitive enjoyment of fire for its own sake, staid and elderly shepherds recapture a forgotten youth. They dart from knoll to knoll with the special paraffin torch, putting up columns of smoke by day and leaving pillars

H

of fire by night, chuckling in the excess of their geniality. The effect of burning on the ground is very marked. A stretch of appetising pale-green hillside bordered by coarse black heather will almost certainly be a " burning," one or two years old.

Some farmers, who live perhaps on islands or whose ground is well ringed with roads, can just touch the heather off and go home : all buildings are well protected by surrounding grass cropped short, and nothing can suffer except maybe fences. Matters are very different near Forestry plantations. A friend of ours was alone on his sheep ground when conditions seemed ideal for burning. He started a small fire. The wind changed, the fire raced into a plantation and he had to face a claim for several thousand pounds. No amount of caution can make heather-burning entirely safe. The rate of progress is, roughly, proportional to the risks taken, and burning therefore brings out nice differences of temperament.

If a small fire were started on a still day on level and uniform ground, the line of flame would form a steadily expanding ring. Once a piece of ground has been burned clean it cannot burn again (at least until there has been further drying or fresh growth), and the only safe place for haversacks and coats to be left is inside the ring. However, the conditions are never so simple. The fire spreads most rapidly up hill, down wind, and in strong heather. The general strategy is to burn first a strip along the edge of any plantation, or across the path that leads to danger. Where possible the strip is curved into a circle. Once the ring is complete, everything within it can be set off, though the edges must be watched for weak places. The cleanest burning is obtained by letting the line of fire advance slowly back into the wind, but speed often calls for a more rough-and-ready burning down wind. Unfortunately it leaves the thicker branches standing to pluck the wool from sheep and to offer forks in which newly-hatched grouse will kill themselves by hanging, which is no fit death for so game a bird.

The worst scares arise when the protective strips are being burned. A line a few yards long is lit. It broadens into two parallel lines, one moving slowly into the wind and the other more rapidly down wind. As soon as it has become separate, the beaters put out the latter fire—if they can. Nine times in ten it is easy. The men beat with special birch brushes and in a few seconds the line is out. The other line is harmless so long as the wind remains constant ; it may be left to eat its way back for a while, or beaten out when the strip is a good safe width. Section by section the strip is carried forward. Matters do not always run so smoothly, however. A gust of wind may convert the sizzling of the lower line into the roar of a furnace. It groans, hisses, snarls. A head of fire races away, perhaps into tall heather or up a slope. Then begins a desperate battle. Owing to the heat the head of the salient cannot be tackled direct. The men must beat their way along the line, extinguishing it as they go, and hoping gradually to catch up on the head. A change in the wind may help, or a burn or a wet patch of bog may halt the break-through. If not, the men must beat away in relays until they do at last catch up ; and everybody keeps an anxious eye on the Forestry fence. Not for nothing are these break-aways called " sweats."

Donald was planning later to put some sheep on Ree Breac, a wide expanse of ground too high for planting and surrounded on three sides by Forestry plantations. Its great defect was that it had no " pass " through the trees down to the Glen. Sudden snow might easily trap the sheep, therefore ; but a pass would mean perhaps a mile of costly deer-fencing. However, the risk was worth taking. The heather had been left to itself for years. Burning would improve its feeding value, and help to anchor the sheep, who are said to smell the new growth on a burning for miles. The anchoring was important as the fourth side is open to all Scotland. Our first day up there was bright and clear. We had one or two sweats, but my initial anxiety faded and I began to enjoy the work. All the world was waiting then for the crisis of the war in Europe, but in the calm of the mountains one had still a fleeting glimpse of the meaning of peace.

Yet the burning itself must be much like a war as seen by military staff. Donald and his brother, home on leave, later finished the strip and then " the squad " burnt out the centre. The line of fire moves slowly and unsteadily across the countryside, leaving black devastation behind it. What slaughter of uncomplaining lives occurs is better not imagined. I saw a frog plop to safety in a peaty pool; and a mouse was caught by one of the dogs, more humane than the fire. There are moles too at this height, and I do not know what other creatures. (Fortunately burning is forbidden after the birds have nested.) And I suppose the struggle to hold a break-through has a military resemblance, too, in a small way.

Later we burnt some of Achbeg hill. The squad first cleared a strip along the edge of Strome Wood. In places the heather was tall and tinder dry. We had our anxious moments. A pointed corner of the plantation projects into the Achbeg hill ground. Some years previously, when Willy was burning, a section had got out of control and jumped into the Forestry. By good luck the accident occurred at the tip of the corner, and the men were able to confine the fire to that triangle. The dead trees are there still, to put fear into the heart of later tenants. It is strange how harmless are the myriads of sparks that are whirled into the air. They give the tiniest stab of pain when they alight on the skin, but do no damage. They never seem to set fire to the driest bent grass. There are, however, other dangers. When a line of fire has been put out, minute flames will lurk unnoticed in hollows, or sphagnum moss will smoulder quietly until the wind reathes life into it. Provided they are noticed immediately these little outbreaks give no trouble; but in a minute or less they may have started a fire there is no holding. Constant alertness is thus needed until all possibility of a flare-up has passed. When the safety belt was finished we burned out several blocks of old heather; and thereafter I could safely put a match to the heather on the Face. I took great care to drive away all sheep at first, but they do not panic and show great commonsense when the fire approaches.

With dipping and clipping, maggot, sales, tupping, heather-burning and lambing we are back at the time of valuations and the wheel of sheep work has come full circle.

CHAPTER VIII

" Is it not strange that sheep's guts should hale souls out of men's bodies ? "—SHAKESPEARE—" Much Ado About Nothing."

The winter nights are much longer in the north than in southern England ; round about Christmas time darkness falls before four o'clock and lasts till well after eight next morning. Winter is accordingly the best time for social life. When all the work that can be done by the light of a storm lantern is finished, there often remains a good long stretch before bedtime for talking, singing and dancing.

Ceilidhs were the real core of social life in the Highlands. The word " ceilidh " is pronounced " caily "—it is a fair specimen of Gaelic spelling—and has come to have two meanings. In London, Glasgow and other haunts of relatively prosperous Highland exiles, the ceilidh is a concert and dance where the musical execution is faultless and everything goes according to plan. Stockbrokers meet with bankers, teachers with shopkeepers, to enjoy the music and to talk wistfully of the heather and the crofts to which they would never think of returning except on holiday. The music and the dances really are the old music and dances, but there the resemblance to a true ceilidh ends.

Spontaneity is the essence of the true ceilidh, the form of which varies according to local custom. Perhaps a few young people will drop in at a neighbour's. There will be talk, light or serious, and refreshments, as in any part of the country, but it is likely enough that there will also be stories, singing and dancing. The children, who will be within earshot whether they have gone to bed or not, will

demand whatever tale is their favourite for the moment—
say, that in which Ian slays the Cailleach by dealing her
a tremendous blow with the head of the Little Man ; and
their half-credulous fear will not prevent them from joining
in with the chanted portions. Then the grandfather may
sing the verses of a song, telling how he first heard it
fifty years ago on the mainland. Time will have taken the
quality from his voice but is unlikely to have dulled his
sense of pitch and of rhythm. The younger people will
join in the chorus, for the songs belong to them as much
as to the oldest. The evening may now take a serious
turn—a discussion on the movements of shoals, or an
argument on the meaning of predestination—or more
probably the young people will dance to their own singing. A half-bottle may be passing from hand to hand
among the men, the womenfolk carefully not seeing it.
At ten or eleven somebody may propose a call on another
family and all agree. The journey may be only a step down
the path, or it may climb over to the next glen, or even a
stiff row out to an island. There may already be callers at
the house when they arrive and the dancers will jostle to
the four walls of the kitchen. If there is no fiddler and no
piper (but on some islands every house has its piper) then
a " mouth-tune " will do. When at last the visitors depart
they may look in to see the new calf, and the cows will
struggle to their feet hoping for their morning sheaf. Such
is one type of ceilidh even to-day in the more isolated
corners.

Outside influences now are killing the ceilidh. There
is a widespread longing for the cinema and the glitter of
shops, a feeling that the world has outgrown home-made
amusements, and everywhere is the insidious " wee boxie "
as Gordon always called it. Though batteries are not
easily re-charged, it is carrying the modern gospel into
every corner. " The Gaelic songs are so dull ! " one boy
said to me. The vitality of an exceptionally vital race is
stored up in them ; strange that they have come to be
thought dull, but such is the fact.

Only at Hogmanay or the New Year does something like the ceilidh become universal now. Christmas is creeping in, and the Old New Year is not quite forgotten, but Hogmanay is the great occasion. We had been warned to have a bottle of whisky ready, and such was the local drouth that we had to get it from England. In former days the whisky ritual was carried to great lengths, and for the first week of the year and more, good men were found in ditches at dawn. Wild stories of such prowess are still heard ; but the habit of moderation has grown and the War brought a merciful shortage. Most families sit up till midnight to see the New Year in, and then begins " first footing." Shortly after midnight there is a rap on the door. A dark man carrying a piece of coal or anything else that is black must be the first to enter. Greetings are exchanged and the host produces his bottle. The men all drink a toast, and the women may take the tiniest sip or join in the good wishes only. So far so good, I thought at our first Hogmanay, but I thought too soon. One of our guests produced his bottle and the toasting was repeated. Tea and scones made a break, and there were songs and joking—and then the third bottle came out. There were as many rounds as bottles, and as many bottles as men ; and this was just a beginning ! No wonder that Gordon was smiling so broadly. Once in ten minutes he would rise to exclaim :

> " Oh, wad some Power the giftie gi'e us,
> To see ourselves as others see us " ;

then he would relapse into ten minutes of benignant silence. After a while we all crossed to Achmore, where a bright fire was waiting. We talked of many things— of poaching, I remember, and of local superstitions. It may have been the same night or the next night that we all linked arms for stability and set out along the Glen. The MacG.'s were asleep, but the fire was quickly relit, more tea and food were offered, and once again the bottles circulated. The more appropriate Gordon's couplet became, the less we saw the point of it. Nobody was drunk, but inhibitions were certainly released and a cordial glow spread through the company. Poems by Burns and others alternated with songs. MacH., who had dropped in, knew many of the songs to the last verse, however long. Everybody contributed something. The best I could offer was " Widdicombe Fair," with other songs equally out-of-place. We all called on Lachlan next door at heaven knows what hour, to find the table spread—and the bottle waiting. So great was the crush that there could be no thought of dancing now, but there was singing galore. Good humour prevailed. In clear, frosty starlight we again linked arms upon the road. I recall the preternatural brightness of the Pleiades caught in a birch-tree while we waited for some laggard. When we parted at the school-house, it must have been very near to milking-time, but nobody minded. Where there are beasts to be tended some work must be done even at Hogmanay, but no other would be thought of at least for the one day.

Later Hogmanays took the same general course, but went with more of a swing—or so it seemed to me. Perhaps the difference was merely that I knew everyone better.

It is worth adding a curious fact. Mackenzie, the historian of the Outer Isles, records that wine was the drink of the Islanders until the seventeenth century, when the brawling and bloodshed that followed the arrival of cargoes led to a strict ban upon the import of wine; thereupon the men took to distilling whisky at home. So little do our beginnings know our ends.

During the first winter we held what was called a singing class, though it quickly developed into something much like a ceilidh. On one night of each week about ten of us met to talk and sing, now at Achmore, now at Achbeg, now at the Forestry Cottage. We had songbooks for the words, but for the most part those who knew a particular song taught those who did not. Several of us did not speak Gaelic, but we found a book of translations (of a sort) to fit the tunes. By good luck several of our company were excellent singers, with a wide knowledge of Highland music and good voices. Scotland is fortunate in having two separate folk-traditions in music, the Lowland which has left a great number of truly national songs, and the Gaelic which may still be alive and developing in a very few places. We sang many Lowland tunes like " The Braes of Balquhidder " and " Sweet Afton " : of these there are scores, even hundreds, widely known still, some poignant, others gay, and nearly all of them alive and beautiful. And we sang many Highland tunes : " Cruachan-Beann," " Crodh Chailein," " Muile nam morbheann " and others. The character of the Gaelic songs varies more widely than that of the others. There are lullabies, hunting songs, love songs and dancing songs. The occupational song is sometimes just a haunting phrase repeated to different words and with variations of rhythm and ornament, in time with the movements of the work. There is no sharp division between vocal and instrumental music, or between singing and dancing. Many of the dance tunes for pipes or fiddle have words by which they are remembered ; and as an old fiddler sweeps and ducks and taps to his playing, his lips will be silently forming the words to help his imagination. Many of the ordinary Gaelic song-tunes dance in one's head, and there are others, the " puirt a beul," that are meant to be dancetunes : a race of enthusiastic dancers will not be deterred by the lack of an instrument. Nobody could hum over " Cairistiona Chaimbeul " (" Christine Campbell ") at high speed without wanting to dance. Once or twice our " class " passed into dancing, when Donald and Moyra sang while the others danced among the furniture.

The movements and steps from which the patterns of Highland dances are built up are highly expressive of grace and energy, and are performed with precision by many of the dancers. The sword-dance is a demonstration piece calling for exceptionally deft movement, but equal vigour goes into the ordinary square dances. In lonely places a dance is a great event, the greater for its rarity. A young man we knew in Argyll would cycle about twenty miles each way on a real Highland track in order to attend a dance, and was not thought exceptional. At the best dances, everybody knows everybody intimately; something like a family feeling develops and the M.C.'s work is then easy. All the men sit along one side of the hall and the women along the other until the next dance is announced. One of the most pleasing features of the dance is the good manners or it. There is no exclusiveness. The younger men see to it that all the women get their share of dancing, including those who protest that their dancing days are past; and like most folk-dances the dances themselves bring several or many couples into the one unit. As the dancers warm up a few coats are shed, and even some waistcoats, ties and collars. For the dancing is no conventionalised walk or slouch; the floor vibrates visibly as forty persons leap or tap simultaneously. Those who are waiting their turn in a square dance join in with movements of hands, feet or body as the mood takes them, and whoop disconcertingly. Friday is the favourite night, since those who do paid work will be having their half-day on the Saturday, and Saturday itself is unthinkably near to the Sabbath. But most of the dancers will have done a full day's work on the Friday, and those who have crofts and families will be as busy on Saturday afternoon as on any other; yet many of them will be up for every dance, from perhaps ten o'clock, a common starting-time, to two or three next morning. The real fun may not begin till midnight.

Everything depends upon the musician, who usually speeds up the pace as each dance progresses and as the evening passes into morning. Faultless execution is not needed, though some of the musicians are excellent performers; it is said that the important thing is that the musician shall be (or shall have been in his day) a keen dancer himself. A terrible cacophany is sometimes introduced when the music is provided by a piano or accordion, which require a knowledge of harmony, for Gaelic music is almost entirely melodic, but the tune and the rhythm sweep away all criticism. Failing all else a gramophone may be employed, but it is inflexible, impersonal and dull. A certain number of modern dances may be mixed in with the reels and schottisches, according to local feeling.

At this point, with the indulgent reader's permission, I will turn aside a little from the narrative, for the subject of Highland dancing brings me very near to the core of our interest in peasant culture. The reader who sees no grounds for indulgence will pass to the next chapter.

The excellence of Highland dancing and singing is not a pure accident. It is due to the survival of a folk-tradition, and has therefore a peculiar importance at the present time. But that importance is not economic, although the folk-arts of Scotland will no doubt be employed as bait for tourist dollars. Nor have the folk-arts the kind of importance attributed to them by revivalists. Certainly folk-songs should be revived in schools, because they are beautiful, easily apprehended, and in tune with the sensibility of the country; moreover they would help to re-create a musical idiom within which conscious artists could carry on their work again. But no revival affects the fundamental problem. If the flowers have withered it is because of far-reaching economic and social changes that can hardly be reversed by any method and certainly not by a folk-revival. There is, for instance, an interesting similarity between the waulking song and Music While You Work, but the difference is still more striking and extends far beyond the quality of the music. When a roll of tweed was finished and ready for waulking, or fulling, the women of a township made a social occasion out of an economic necessity. They sat at a long trestle table, passing the wet cloth backwards and forwards across the table, and singing in time with the different movements required. Interestingly enough, they concluded with a blessing on the future wearer. To-day factories are being fitted up with loudspeakers, and music from records or from the wireless receiver is made to drown the noise of the machinery. The intention is much the same as with the waulking, to relieve the tedium of a repeated movement and to speed up production. For the rest, the two situations typify the difference between two worlds. It is not only the aesthetic difference that stands out, though that is plain enough to anyone with a jot of musical taste. It would be all to the good if workers could be persuaded to listen to " Spanish Ladies " instead of " Your ruby lips give me the blues," but no spanner would be raised in benediction. The musical initiative, like the economic initiative, would still come from above. The area of effective choice from minute to minute and from day to day is far less in the case of the factory worker. He cannot make even the most elementary decisions about his work. In Mr. Ford's factories, " no man uses more than one tool, all the work comes waist high, a man never has to stoop or to move his feet to get anything, and the speed of the work is controlled not by the worker's will but by the pace of the conveyor." The decisions that alter the course of his life are made, not under his own roof, but in Fleet Street, Wall Street, and places he never heard of.

Hence I do not share the hopes of revivalists. Moreover it must be admitted that some strange people cluster round the folk-arts at present. Here, for instance, is part of a song, as translated by one of them :

" If you heard my pretty
One singing her ditty,
Your bosom would get in a blaze, a blaze."

This is plain vulgarity when all allowance has been made for the difficulty of verse translation. There is also the " lilt of grail-deeds " school, and that of the good-living kilted Highlander whose only beverage is goat's milk. Escapism, emotional vehemence, and sentimental gush invite ridicule that is very willingly extended to folk art itself. It is natural that anything so disturbing should be laughed out of countenance. For the relics of the folk-arts *are* profoundly disturbing. Just as the intellectual equanimity of an earlier generation was broken by a few geological fossils, our own ease of mind would be ended by the challenge of those aesthetic fossils, the relics of folk-art. It is the more necessary to state the nature of the challenge. What is true of folk-song is true, *mutatis mutandis*, of the other forms of art—Fair-Isle knitting, the patterns of tweed, the proportions of buildings, and so on ; but owing to the ease with which recorded songs may be studied from the many excellent publications now obtainable, I will speak mostly of the songs.

There are three outstanding facts about folk-song, that it is popular, that it is beautiful and that it is precarious.

It is popular to an exceptional degree, in that it is the expression of the people, by the people, for the people. When Strauss's tunes were whistled by errand-boys they still were less popular than folk-song because they sprang from one individual. Folk-song, a truly composite art, is the working of a long process of mutation and selection. Doubtless some musically gifted person in a community provided the nucleus of a song. It would be imperfectly remembered by the singer himself and by his hearers, who would repeat it later with unconscious modifications. Some of the modifications would " catch on " better than others, and the new version would undergo further modifications. In the absence of any written version to which the singers could refer, there would be a cumulative variation that would change the whole nature of the song in the course of time. The variations would not be wholly random, as they would be influenced by the singer's taste, and there would also be a constant trend or bias in the process of selection, owing to the distinctive taste of the community as a whole. Where communication between two districts was fairly difficult, two versions would develop ; and there could be no " final " version so long as the tradition remained purely aural. The interplay of external environment and a living force has produced the variety of forms studied in biology ; the horse's hoof and the seal's flipper may be said to reflect the conditions of plain and sea. In folk-song, both the musical urge and the controlling choice, corresponding to the living force and to environment, come from the people themselves. It is therefore more than a reflection, it is the direct expression of the temperament of a given people. As soon as there is a standard of reference, further development is halted. The song is embalmed. But for the work of Cecil Sharp and other distinguished collectors, most of the English songs would by now have passed into oblivion, but at an earlier stage similar work would actually have been fatal to the songs. The growth of literacy, including musical literacy, has removed one of the conditions necessary for a developing folk-art. Here again revivals are merely scratching on the surface.

The first fact about folk-art, that it is uniquely popular, would be of no importance but for the second, that it is extremely beautiful. For many years I have taken every opportunity of becoming familiar with examples of folk-art, and am acquainted with a considerable number of songs. Some of them have proved dull and uninspired, but in my judgment (for what it is worth) not one specimen has been ugly or banal or anything worse than neutral. There is more plain, deliberate ugliness concentrated in the borough of St. Pancras than in the whole of peasant Europe. (I am speaking at the moment only of aesthetic ugliness, of course.) The Highland milking tune " Bo Lurach Thu " is a lovely song, subtle, controlled, yet full of an insistent energy. But so too is " Leezie Lindsay " ; so is " Searching for Lambs." So are a thousand songs from many countries.

The character of folk-music is blurred by the normal manner of presentation to-day. Gaelic music must be heard in its true setting if it is to be appreciated. I am not referring to the pounding of Atlantic breakers and the scent of peat-smoke, but to the strictly musical conditions. Though there have been some authentic broadcasts, most wireless and gramophone renderings give a false impression. The songs are accompanied, or sung in harmonised versions by concert-trained voices. It is

especially the tone-production that is wrong. The performers are taught to aim at a rich or mellow tone, where
the songs require a much thinner, more astringent quality
of voice. The difference is as great as that between flute
and clarinet. We had formed this impression before a
Skye girl, herself a fine singer, told us she thought the
wireless programmes quite wrong in their approach. A
training in plainsong would be at least equally appropriate—some of the songs are in the medieval modes
and usually not in the modern scales at all—but custom
without conscious training is the best guide. And an
accompaniment, especially when it is percussive, alters
the whole character of the melody, much of which derives
from grace notes single or grouped. It is useless for the
singer to glide rapidly over two notes to a third that will
receive greater duration but not greater stress, if a chord
from the piano blunders in on the third note. The illusion of a birdlike wildness is rudely ended by the thump.
Variety is provided by the alternation of the choruses,
which are taken in unison, and the verses taken solo.
Executed thus the songs have a primitive beauty that
recalls Indian and African music rather than " The
Beggar's Opera." They are the expression of a lively
sensibility in close touch with realities ; there is in the
texture of them the musical equivalent of sparkle, or an
acuity of the five senses.

Folk-art, then, is popular and it is beautiful ; it is also
remarkably precarious. It depends upon a directness and
simplicity of outlook that are readily undermined. Cecil
Sharp records that English folk-song died about the
middle of the last century—that the songs were unknown
to villagers born after, say, 1840 ; when collecting songs
he had to go to the old people who had learned them in
their youth. In Scotland the inner story is much the
same, though the revival movement has occurred there
while the songs are still remembered. The values of
industrial society acquire a tremendous prestige in the
eyes of more primitive societies. How could it be other-

Achmore and Achbeg. A few houses, and then miles of open hill.

Potato-sorting. It can be pleasant or dull work, but hardly exciting.

Fernaig hill in winter. The snow brings out unnoticed ledges and hollows.

Fernaig hill in summer. Sheep on the ledges had sometimes to be rescued with ropes, or even shot.

wise ? When the fishing-smack is hopelessly outclassed by the trawler and the hand-loom by the power-loom, who will pause to reflect that technical proficiency may go with spiritual incoherence ? The clothes, habits, songs, language and outlook of Hollywood reveal a new Promised Land to the five continents. As the power of money advances, that of song recedes.

Good music is still composed and the good music of the past is still performed, but they concern a minority only. Thousands attended the National Gallery concerts during the War ; millions did not. There is an almost complete cleavage between classical and popular music, and practically no cross-communication. Indeed there is active hostility, implied in such terms as " highbrow " and " lowbrow." However invidious the task, two things must be said about modern popular music.

First, its quality is utterly deplorable. The charge against it is not, as its supporters care to believe, that it is too lively, but that it is dead. Words and tunes alike betray an atrophy of the five senses, an inability to make contact with reality.

> " Everybuddy loves ma bebby,
> But ma bebby don't love nobuddy but me,"

or again—

> " Our lovely love affair
> ·Will make the neighbours stare,
> And say, There goes (sic) the Joneses, what a pair ! "

This is not life ; it is death—the death of the intellect, of the moral sense, of the whole sensibility. Very little popular music to-day is better than neutral. Its affinities are not with healthy instinct but with pornography. It stirs up and dwells upon feelings that can find no external objective. Much of it is merely conventionalised whining and moaning. It is the expression of a slave mentality and some of the rhythms—the more lively ones—do in fact derive from slave music. For all its apparent slickness and sophistication, it is at heart, " weary, stale, flat and unprofitable."

I

Second, the decline in popular taste is a matter of enormous importance. Man has compelling material needs and his energies upon earth are directed largely towards their satisfaction. But deeper and equally compelling needs crave for satisfaction along with them. He is not fundamentally a consumer, nor even a pleasure-seeker, for the deliberate pursuit of pleasure is self-defeating. Political realists nowadays scoff at the notion that he is fundamentally a seeker after goodness, truth and beauty, and yet these are, widely interpreted, the only objects the pursuit of which knows no satiety. Truth, in the limited sense of scientific truth, is in good hands, though it has little direct meaning to the great number of mankind, and goodness is outside the immediate discussion. The negation of beauty is the negation of life. " If I may make the songs of a people, I care not who makes its laws "—this amounts to an over-statement of a truth. Interest in the aesthetic quality of living is no luxury, it is one of the first and last necessities. Bad art is bad living ; it is wasteful and destructive, whether the final judgment is made in qualitative, religious terms or purely in quantitative terms. " Not that which goeth into the mouth defileth a man ; but that which cometh out of the mouth, this defileth a man." Hence the war against Want, Disease, Ignorance, Squalor and Idleness, urgent though it may be, cannot be allowed to absorb the whole of our attention. To put aside considerations of taste until the more urgent battles are won is to abandon them altogether, for the choice of means deflects and may even determine the ultimate choice of ends. Who will decide when the battles have been won ? Is there any reason to suppose that they will ever be considered at an end ? Materialism may be a respectable doctrine at the philosophical level, but at the level of everyday practical affairs it leads to the *indefinite* amassing of material goods, to the notion, already familiar, of an *indefinitely* rising standard of living. One objection to material accretion is that satisfaction falls off so rapidly. Whereas the discovery of a new idea or a new song may be equally engrossing whether it is the first, the second or the thousandth, a house with eight rooms does not give twice the satisfaction given by a house with four; and when I see branded confections stuffed into the mouths of pasty-faced infants, I wonder whether any net satisfaction is being derived at all.

There is only one way of influencing popular taste in the future, that of influencing it now. What can be done? There are, I believe, two mistaken answers to the question.

The first mistake is to leave everything to education. Some people are of the opinion that the gulf between the taste of the many and the taste of the few is due entirely to the fact that the many are " culturally under-privileged." Given enough teachers with enough enthusiasm and enough equipment, the many could be won over to the tastes of the few. It is certainly true that a considerable number of conversions could be made; they are being made to-day in schools, in the W.E.A., and in many organisations, and there must be few avocations in which success is more exhilarating. But there is a statistical side to the problem. It is not enough to win over the administrators, managers and foremen—and teachers—to a liking for the classics, nor even a certain few of the " other ranks "—the metal-workers, shop-assistants, miners, farm-labourers, textile-workers, housewives, and others who comprise the tens of millions of adults in this country. To be deemed successful the teachers' campaign would have to win over the great majority of these humbler people. The classics (say, " The Waste Land " and the Brandenburg Concertos) will *never* be made popular in this wider context even if the National Debt is doubled in the attempt. They have not the qualities necessary to popular art. Whoever believes that

> " Why then Ile fit you.   Hieronymo's mad againe.
> Datta.   Dayadhvam.   Damyata.
> Shantih shantih shantih "

can be made to drive out " Workers' Playtime " is flattering the teaching profession. Farmers are in no way contemptuous of sows' ears, but they do not confuse them with material for silk purses.

The contrary mistake is to suppose that the " profanum vulgus " is inherently devoid of taste, actual or potential, and that matters were always so, will always be so, and are best left to take their course. Popularity is vulgarity to-day. The identity is permanent, the argument runs, and the sows' ears deserve at most our condescension. It happens that there is a complete refutation to this widely-held belief. The significance of the folk-arts is that they cut right across the popular-classical division ; they render the highbrow-lowbrow opposition meaningless. In a folk culture there is no need to win the many over to the tastes of the few : the artists come willingly to the many for their themes and their inspiration. Folk-song, though uniquely popular, is allied in quality to the greatest " highbrow " music ; it has supplied the motifs of some of the most " classical " compositions. The only use of modern popular song in art-music that I can recall occurs in " Façade," where the intention is ironical. How could it be otherwise ? Yet the present state is not the norm, it is an exception that may have no precedent in the history of civilisation. The supreme importance of the folk-arts to-day is the proof they offer that cultural vacuity is not the inevitable lot nor even the usual lot of the many who cannot master the classics. Modern society has changed so much that the folk-arts have lost their direct relevance ; but if it cannot develop an *equivalent* popular culture, then the fault lies with modern society and not with the endowment of ordinary human beings.

Here, then, is the more immediate challenge of the folk-arts. If man is fundamentally a maker of patterns, the folk-arts were remarkably effective patterns. There is a second and wider significance. After language itself, they are the clearest example of the power of a living tradition. It is hardly conceivable that individuals chosen at random, and acting purely as individuals, could compose music nearly so distinguished as the average Gaelic tune.

In some fashion folk-art succeeds in placing at the disposal of each individual, not only the best experience of his superiors, but also that of earlier generations. It would be difficult to over-emphasise the importance of these two extensions of the faculties of the individual—they are the essence of a tradition, and the lack of any tradition is at the root of much contemporary bewilderment. " There is no excuse for any literate person if he is less than three thousand years old in mind," writes Capt. Liddell Hart in " Why Don't We Learn from History ? " There is a corresponding need in other than intellectual matters, and for other than highly literate persons. We have, it is true, cast off the restraint of over-rigid traditions, but at a high cost. Each of us must start " from scratch," as though history had never been lived.

The break in continuity with the past would be of less importance if we had retained the other feature of a living tradition, that is, if our society were so organised that the best contemporary elements had the predominance. That is the reverse of what happens. The more clever or astute members of society vie for the support of the multitude. They cannot use compulsion, and their competition (whether political or commercial) must take the form of an elaboration of quick appeals. There is every encouragement for the first thought rather than the second, the crude emotion rather than the refined. As Sir Norman Angell has said, had Lord Northcliffe run his papers on more responsible lines, he would not have been Lord Northcliffe. Twenty years ago Sir Norman described the predicament of the modern journalist in a pamphlet (" The Press and the Organization of Society ") that has only grown more apposite with the passing of time. His words are equally applicable to many other matters than journalism, and may the more usefully be quoted because he is no sentimental revivalist. " Just as in commerce debased coin, if there be enough of it, must drive out the sterling, so in the contest of motives, action which responds to the more primitive feelings and impulses, to

first thoughts and established prejudices, can be stimu-
lated by the modern newspaper far more easily than that
prompted by rationalised second thought. Any newspaper appealing to the former group of motives must
' get away with it ' long before one which appeals to the
second can establish its case. . . . We get the operation of
that Gresham Law under which the more reflective and
ratiocinated type of opinion must be driven out by the
more emotional. Modern conditions of industry and
finance tend to increase this premium upon the more
impulsive and dangerous type of policy."

Here is the most significant contrast between folk
society and modern industrial society. It is plain that
the beauty of the folk-arts is the result of a process of
levelling-up. They are not merely the *reflection* or *expression*
of a communal taste ; they are also an active educative
influence in the formation of that taste. Somehow it is
the good currency that drives out the bad. To-day, on
Sir Norman's analysis, we have brought about the opposite effect. There is a levelling down. In a given situation
it is not the wisest counsel or the most beautiful version
that will prevail, but that which can strike home first.
Thus the less scrupulous of those who should be leaders
are driven to exploiting the weakness of " the masses,"
and the more scrupulous retire into the isolation of the
highbrow. Those who set up as the protagonists of the
masses unknowingly pay them the poorest compliment.
" My own staff," writes Mr. A. S. Neill, " may sometimes
wear sandals, but they are all known at the local pub and
the local tobacconist. In short, they are in touch with the
larger crowd we call humanity." The sandal here is, it
seems, a localised expression of general enlightenment, and
contact between the enlightened and the larger crowd is
rightly recommended. What is interesting is the assumption that it is only possible at the beer-and-tobacco level ;
the simple pleasures of the poor, we are to believe, do
not rise above froth-blowing. In Mr. Neill's home country
there are at least relics of a more fertile intercourse. The

existence of a folk-tradition sets up a vital connection between the members of a community. It is not a substitute for contact between individuals, but it helps to make that contact fruitful. When it is lacking, inner loneliness, a far more damaging thing than geographical loneliness, drives the enlightened down to a beery camaraderie, and drives whole nations to the synthetic unity of the totalitarian state.

There are thus two contrary errors; the one is to suppose that " the larger crowd " can be won over to the classics; the other is to give it credit for no higher tastes than tippling, betting and Blackpool.

The first task is to get social relations altered, to re-establish genuine communication between the " enlightened " and " the crowd," to remove the stratification of society; and the first step is certainly to recognize the problem. Nobody who had heard something of Hebridean music, heard it with his ears and his mind wide open, would be content with the pessimistic objective of bringing the highbrows round into the public bar. It was unlettered women singing in the byres of a " backward " island who composed " Bo Lurach Thu "; yet I doubt if any living musician would claim to have written a better tune.

I became without intention an eavesdropper when waiting, for a bus of all things, on a lonely stretch of road across a bog. The only shelter being a but and ben at the road junction, I leant against the wall, out of sight of the windows. A woman was singing within. From the domestic thumps and the sound of small children it was plain that she was singing at her housework. None of her songs was then known to me and I had hardly any Gaelic; but they had the delicacy and the almost overpowering poignancy with which I have since become more familiar. She was an excellent singer, her voice seeming to embody rather than to interpret the music. I have never observed in a concert hall so complete an identification of the voice and the song, such a complete unconsciousness of self. At one point the door opened and some water was thrown out. Perhaps I should have pitied her for the lack of a sink. Plumbing is a useful thing. But music is an end in itself where plumbing is only a means. The unhappy fact about much of industrial England is that it has killed the music without providing the plumbing.

It is not remarkable to stumble upon such music in the Highlands, but it would be strange in the south. I have been present at a good number of sing-songs at clubs, hostels, camps and football-matches. They are interesting enough as an ebullition of high-spirits, and in some cases as a manifestation of group solidarity, but as music they are negligible. Yet a sing-song can be very moving. There is one that remains with great vividness in my mind. For once the Minch was in a quiet mood. In the curved saloon in the stern of the " Lochnevis," a number of young men and women were passing away the night by singing. They were Hebrideans returning to the mainland after a spell of leave from the Forces. Two of the girls sang particularly well. If one of them was taking a verse, she would close her eyes, and rock her head in time to the beat of the music, while the others swayed slightly, and at the end of each verse they would take up the chorus in perfect unison. There was no fumbling, no hesitation ; all were on their own ground. And once again there was the identification of the music with the voices. I had the sensation that I was hearing not a few men and women on leave, nor even a generation, but a whole race, past and present. The songs were not that year's fashion. They had been known by the singers almost from their cradles ; they had been learned by them from the old people, who themselves had learned them perhaps when the threatened invader was a Napoleon. Wordsworth felt that the rainbow gave continuity to his life through childhood, manhood and age ; the folk-arts are the medium of a much wider continuity. On that still evening, when so much of the world was reverberating to high-explosive, the voices of men and women long dead joined with the voices of the living through a tradition that had not yet died.

But its days are numbered. How many, I wonder, of the singers will ever return to the Islands?

CHAPTER IX

" If heraldry were guided by reason, a plough in a field arable
would be the most noble and ancient coat of arms."

A. COWLEY—" Essays."

The occasion on which Gaelic music moved me most
deeply was neither a dance nor a ceilidh, but a funeral
I attended during the first winter. The service here takes
place at the door of the cottage, and the cottage in this
case happened to be at the very edge of the sea-shore.
Gaelic psalm-tunes were sung in the haunting old versions
of the Gaelic people themselves—versions which often
resemble English hymn-tunes in their general contour,
but which, embellished with the characteristic grace-notes
and taken very slowly, suggest quite another world.
Shadows of screaming gulls flashed over the bare heads
of the men and a heron watched from a distance. The
gaunt Applecross hills, where snow still lay on the heights
and in the gullies, the humble cottage by the water, and
the perfect dignity of those most affected, belonged one
to another. Life and death will be like this, and grief will
be so expressed, when New York and London have
crumbled. After the psalms the coffin was carried up the
steep lane, all the men taking their turn at the bier out of
respect for the dead. There are no wakes now to help
the relatives over the first impact of a death, but the
women of the Glen still pay formal calls on the bereaved
wife or mother. In lonely places there is time for the
decencies of living whatever the season.

But work presses, at all seasons. There is, of course,
a winter respite after the full pressure of work at hay,
corn and potatoes, and there is time for the social arts ;
but the notion that crofters take an unbroken nap from

November to March is far from the truth. The winter is surprisingly short and busy. This first winter we were still at the potatoes in December, and preparations for spring work must begin just as soon as the worst of the weather is over. And during winter itself there is plenty of work to be done.

First there are sheep. The tups are on the hill until early January, and a watch must be kept for sheep in snowdrifts, or sheep on their backs and unable to regain their legs.

Then there is the daily routine of cattle work, which takes up much time in winter. During the colder months the cattle are nearly all kept in at night; on the very worst days, too, when sleet or snow cause them to stand miserably without grazing, they are put out only for a drink and then back into the byre, where their energy can be employed to better purpose than in warming Scotland. Though we did not normally start very early, the first work was done by starlight (the constellations always looked topsy-turvy and unseasonable to me on winter mornings) or by the light of a storm-lantern. Corn—later in the season hay—must be carried and the day's threshing done. I enjoyed the threshing: monotonous yet rhythmical, it is one of the many kinds of work that are pleasant in short spells but would be drudgery over long periods. Certainly I preferred my daily quota of beating away with a hazel stick to the days of subjection to the travelling thresher earlier—though the machine admittedly threshes the corn much cleaner. Prince too must be fed and groomed and his stable mucked-out. When D. had finished milking, the cows received their ration of a sheaf or more, according to circumstances, and any extras, and then we went in to breakfast. When the cows had been put out on to the hill or driven to their grazing for the day, there was the daily wrestle with the cobbles. For the byre and stable floors and the " grip " itself were set with small cobbles, and the apron outside with much larger ones. Cobbles have the merit, and that a great one on a croft, that they cost nothing : they lie on the shore waiting to be carried away for flooring. It is their only merit. They are the most labour-creating device in the world. The wheel of our metal barrow was soon shaken to pieces. I mended the wheel and then the steel of the body tore, actually tore, under the strain. We should certainly have cemented the floor and the apron had Achbeg been our own—but that is too large a subject to open up here. Then the hay or straw was put in ready for evening, and the turnips, chat potatoes or other food put into the buckets. The cattle needed no urging homewards at evening. The thought of the buckets and the warm byre always drew them to the gate. The race when the gate opened kept only a slight semblance of dignity, and Cheetah always finished by breaking into an open gallop. There was the evening milking to be done, and straw often to be carted from the borrowed barn, and countless smaller jobs like sawing logs and clearing drains. All of this routine work I liked well enough : it occupied one's body and something of one's mind, and had a fair amount of variety. My one complaint was that it absorbed so much time that could have been spent in the fields. A good deal of this work we did, of course, outside the hours of daylight.

We managed well enough in the byre and in the house by paraffin-light, and even, when oil ran out, by candle-light. Much is being made of the present electrification of the Highlands, but if it is not accompanied by a conscious policy of decentralisation of industry I am afraid the chief effect will be to enable radio to kill the spontaneous life of the region a little more quickly. In the house, electricity is a convenience but by no means a necessity. Lights do not need to be carried around, and your sewing or your paper does not need to be so close to the lamp ; that is about all. It is true that electricity saves work, but it also costs money, and you must work harder to earn that extra money ; and when you have worked harder prices may slump and then you may not have the extra money, but you will have the bill just the same ; and then . . . ? In the days when candles were expensive, whale-oil scarce, and paraffin unknown here, the chief light in the long evenings must have been the glow of the peat-fire ; a light insufficient for most work, but one that must have drawn people together and encouraged the arts of song, story and conversation. It is in the steading that better lighting would be a real convenience. For sorting potatoes or tending a sick calf paraffin lamps are inadequate. When feeding cattle after dark I used to clasp bundles of sheaves to bring them from barn to byre, and stumble across the cobbles with the lantern swinging from a finger beyond the bundle. A whiff of burning arose whenever a straw poked inside the lamp-glass, and I often wondered just how suddenly the bundle, helped by the paraffin that sometimes slopped on to it, would flare up if it once started. Provided every object is in its familiar place, and the familiar round is not disturbed by untoward happenings, it is possible to do a surprising amount of work in complete darkness—chaining cows, foddering, even the milking. When putting hay into the heck after the cows are in, you become painfully aware just how utterly exposed your stomach is to the horns of the unseen cow. You acquire a sixth sense—perhaps it is the perception of reflected or radiated heat—that tells you pretty accurately where and how the animals are standing. I recall minor mishaps. One evening, rummaging in the manger for the stall-halter, I inadvertently put my hand into the particular morsel Prince was about to bite ; and if that accidental nip is any guide, I should rather be kicked than bitten by an angry horse. On another occasion, when reaching for his bridle, I ran my fingers over an enormous denture—he was yawning silently in the dark. And there was also the occasion when Prince and I, coming in very late, walked full into the bony rear of a cow. Pursuing what are, I understand, called intruder methods, a strange cow had followed our own into the steading, and finding no empty stall in the byre had settled down in the stable to enjoy Prince's evening meal. There is, finally, a risk in letting cows into a dark byre. Normally they go straight to their places—in even the largest cowshed, all the Buttercups and Daisies walk unfalteringly to their respective stalls—knowing exactly what to expect and where ; but if something is wrong, a bucket forgotten, perhaps, or a kitten in the manger, the blackness becomes a scuffling, roaring turmoil into which you plunge at your risk. On such occasions I did sigh for a handy switch.

Then there is work with the cattle other than the purely routine work. Cheetah, for instance, calved suddenly and without due warning in the snow, without harm to herself or the calf, luckily. We fed the calf from the bucket for three weeks, after which I took it to the sale in Dingwall. It was a bull calf and sold well. The calf had to go because milk had become very scarce over the winter. Unable to find another suitable cow for sale, we had already borrowed a cross-Ayrshire, Jean, for the winter: it is a common arrangement, by which the borrower has the milk in return for wintering. Jean had kept us going, but by the time Cheetah calved we were again having difficulty in meeting our commitments. We therefore decided to take the calf Prima off Maundy and to milk Maundy for the rest of her lactation. We expected difficulty, and were not disappointed. Our plan was to draw off some milk from Maundy, teach the calf to drink once more, wean it, and then change it over gradually to milk-equivalent or other such food in place of the milk. Maundy, however, was in no mood to help. An hour of pumping produced not a saucerful. Later in the day she gave us a little, but we had to let the calf have the rest direct. The days that followed saw a battle of wills, with no very clear outcome. Sometimes she let down and sometimes she did not. When she let down, milk spurted abundantly from the severed teat, so that this became an index of her inclination. We lost countless hours cajoling, massaging and threatening ; I even tried milking-croons. Eventually she resigned herself to her status as a milker, but was always apt to hold back now and then. Prima too was difficult ;

she refused to drink. She knew a far better way of feeding and resented our interference. We succeeded, by letting her become very hungry : over Maundy we had no equivalent hold.

Very little peat was cut in the Glen, partly because the cutting and drying steal so much time from haymaking and partly because the best peat is exhausted. Our own peat hag was at the most inaccessible part of the farm, up by Creag Mheaol. Instead of peat, wood is cut now. There were full-grown alders and skeleton oaks ringed to kill them at the time the conifers were planted ; but chiefly we cut the birch trees that are gradually over-running the lower hills. It was warm work for days when snow halted most other work. We felled the larger trees, snedded them, dragged bundles of trunks down to the road behind Dicky and Prince, and piled them over the carts. Birch burns with a pleasant flicker.

Then there was seaweed to cart. A simple form of composting has long been practised here on the West. Seaweed is spread upon the midden layer by layer as the midden grows throughout the winter, and is thus thoroughly mixed with the manure when that goes out to the fields in spring. Seaweed is also spread on the young grass. This must be done early in the winter, so that there will be no hard strands to clog the mower knife next summer. The fertile soil at Portachullin shore has, I suspect, been largely formed from accumulated seaweed carried laboriously in creels on to the pebbly ground by generations of crofters and their families.

In addition to the lines of clean seaweed brought in by westerly storms, a large bank of half-rotted deciduous leaves had been formed, brought down, no doubt, by the Ascaig and carried in again by tidal currents. Since only rather small loads could be taken up the steep brae at the shore, we made a pile by the road there, and later took much larger loads up past the Falls to our two farms. We usually worked together, one on the load and one forking. At times we cut seaweed at low tide, loading it direct on to the carts. In former days the men and women used to lash together huge rafts of seaweed, and tow them at a spring tide close to their strips of ground. Sometimes a warm winter sun kept the horses quiet here, but usually there was a stinging wind and often heavy showers of rain and hail. Squalls snatched the seaweed from our graips and flung it far over and beyond the carts. Prince hated the wind, and the treacherous feel of the pebbles under his hoofs. We had to keep our dogs close at heel because of the trains that thundered past on the curving track. There was one day an accident to another dog that led Donald to tell me of a curious custom now extinct. It seems that the skin of a dog can be made thoroughly watertight. When a dog died, therefore, its skin was removed with the least possible amount of cutting, inflated and sewn tight, and used as a fishing-float. It is eerie to think of a bearded crofter-fisherman, alone at his nets in the silent night, with his old favourites bobbing in the water around him.

A sideline which took up a very considerable amount of time, especially in winter, must be mentioned here ; the carting of coal. The stationmaster kept a stock of coal for retailing, but as he had no lorry or cart, most of the coal for the Glen and Stromeferry was taken out by Dicky and Prince.

This coal-carting had a very pleasant side to it and a very irritating one, and I am tempted to say much about it. The pleasant side was the work itself. First half a ton of coal was heaved into the cart. This is just a stretch for the muscles—very different from the *continuous* shovelling for long spells I had watched in Norfolk. If the flies were bad, or an engine standing in the siding ready to make one of its nameless noises, I had to watch Prince pretty closely ; otherwise he stood perfectly. Next, we went round over the big bridge to the weighbridge. A few words, perhaps, with Colin Mor, the ferryman, or with someone waiting for the Goods. The rest was just walking, and whatever the weather I enjoyed it.

Applecross. It was against the islands of the foreground loch that the boat from Plockton might have driven.

Carrie. Well-fed and enjoying the winter sunshine.

The Face. Gathering sheep on ground like this can be very heavy on the dogs.

Achbeg house. The birches beyond are slowly regaining possession of the hillsides, as there are now few cattle to trample the seedlings.

When in good strip, Prince could pull his sixteen hundredweight gross up the brae, from sea-level to the shoulder, without asking for a pause, but I always made him rest where the road permitted. Often towards night his hoofs would strike flashes out of the road metal. And once when the calkers had worn from his shoes, he lost his grip on the steepest part of the brae. There followed an alarming backsliding that was hard to guide and impossible to check, though we finished against a bank without disaster. The brae once surmounted he would settle to the brisk pace that is just right for man and horse in an east wind. If the day were wet and stormy and oilskins working well, it was easy enough to shut out the world and retire into one's own thoughts ; though a trickle down the spine usually insinuated itself in the end. One need never be lonely with a horse. Prince would peer into the quarries where a lurking sheep had once startled him, he would insist on his drink at the well, neigh to Dick and Shula, and halt at his own unvarying spots for his own purposes. Every season—every week almost—had something new to keep the five wits alive and interested. Silky tufts of cotton-grass might be quivering under the whining telegraph wires. In summer there were stone-chats in the hawthorn at the head of the Brae ; always there were meadow-pippets with their bounding flight and their ecstatic little " peep-peep," and from high overhead the sonorous detached croak of the raven. Freaks of air-currents, which the stalker knows so well, might keep two layers of cloud scudding in opposite ways on the Lochcarron hillside, or it might be the healthy green just breaking on the burning that caught my eye. I loved to watch the slow wheeling of the fields and the houses as we came obliquely down into the Glen. And along the shore, if the load took me that way, there were thickets of briars in flower or in berry, seaweed, sea-birds, and the changes of the sea itself. Sometimes the Coolins would stare harshly across the water, white snow and black rock ; sometimes they would soften to Quaker grey. Quite often a false sky would

K

hide every trace of them. When the coal was couped, there might be, if the time were near Hogmanay, a glass of whisky; and one particularly bleak day who should come to meet me on the green by the shore but Katey with a sheaf for Prince and a cup of hot soup for me.

Then perhaps I could time my next journey so as to watch the Mail train go through the station. The railway has a great fascination in such lonely places. After Post—who was himself dependent on the railway—it was our chief link with the outside world. The mere passing of a train over the embankment at the mouth of the Glen turned our thoughts for a moment from our own small world to the world along the line. Trains on the embankment were visible from many of our fields, and audible from them all. When we were stooping over potatoes at planting, or over sheep at the fank, a train would slide by and backs would be gratefully straightened for a moment. "Ah, that'll be the Mail," or "Ah, that'll be the Early Goods," someone would say.—"M-hm."—A few moments' speculation based on the number and type of trucks or the lateness of the train, and then backs would bend again to the task. The passing of the evening train is a social occasion. Knots of young people gather at the stations to see it go through, finding perhaps something of the interest of a film in the flickering compartments. A sailor absorbed in a comic—flash—a too-loving couple—flash—a Minister all unsuspecting—a game of poker—a Pekingese—an Air-Marshal— . . . Then a chat with the guard and the latest news from all along the line. Distemper at Portree; herring at Kishorn; better news of Sandy McH. A hoot and the train glides out into the unknown. The evening's show is over but it has always brought something of interest.

But I was speaking of coal-carting. It was, I have said, as leisurely and enjoyable a way of getting through the day as anyone could wish.

There were, moreover, many neighbours whose coals I would have been glad to cart without payment; my debt to them was more that I could have repaid in this way.

But—there is, of course, a but to this idyll. One's economic self will slip in a " but " at the end of every idyll.

Whether carting " paid " depends on how you look at it. I had to keep a horse and cart in any case. For days on end Prince would eat his fill in idleness while tufts of grass sprouted from the cracks in the woodwork of the cart. Carting therefore brought in something at negligible cost—a handful of extra feed for Prince and maybe a scraping of cart-grease on the axle. I could regard it as almost pure profit as railway companies are said to regard the fares brought in by an excursion train.

Carting, however, is very slow work. The longest of my journeys was that from the station to Portachullin, both of them at sea-level and barely half a mile apart. There was no way of getting a cart along the shore or along the railway line. Instead, Prince had to haul his load up the Brae to a height of 300 feet, round by Achbeg and Fernaig, and back along the pebbly track by the shore's edge, say three miles in all. The double journey could not be done in less than three hours, but there were always delays that brought it nearer to four. Whenever possible I took up a load of pebbles or seaweed from the beach, or potatoes to Strome, but it was usually necessary to travel empty one way. Hence the full charge for such a journey would work out at well above ten shillings—far more than anyone would think of asking.

Thus carting took up time that I should have liked to spend in other ways—particularly in attempting to improve the arable by composting, liming heavily and draining. A year's carting brought in just what an average three-weeks'-old calf would fetch in the ring. If, therefore, I could have used the time to make our ground carry two extra calves, that would have been a more profitable use of the time. True, the perfect crofter would have managed both the carting and the calves—but I didn't.

In addition to the cattle work, carting, etc., there was

the potato sorting to be done. It could be disheartening work if you were alone at the pit and the east wind was coming down from the snows of Ben Kilillan ; it was coldest of all on the windy, slightly wet days that reduce your fingers to a bundle of clothes-pegs ; but with good company and with the February sun upon your back it could be pleasant enough. The tubers had to be sorted into three sizes, those for eating, those for seed, and the remainder, which went to our own hens and those of neighbours, and also, if there were enough, to the cattle. Cattle and horses love potatoes best of all foods. At times we were obliged to leave potatoes in the byre or the stable, but I never slept soundly for as long as they were there. Animals were always working loose, and were apt to reach the potatoes. Maundy was so clever at slipping the chain over her poll that I had to tie her with a halter (and even this she would systematically rub against her stall, working it inch by inch towards her snout). When a cow comes at a pile of potatoes it gorges itself until its stomach swells. If you are quick enough in pushing a pointed tube into just the right spot in her side you may save her life. We had many narrow escapes ; cattle tore open bags of potatoes or broke down barriers, but they were always discovered in time, and I never had to perform that alarming operation.

The ware potatoes were sold locally at a controlled price ; owing to the inaccessibility of the area we were not subject to the ordinary requisitioning of potato stocks. The potatoes of seed size were kept for the coming crop ; and, in spite of good intentions every winter, we were seldom ready with all our seed much before the work of preparing the ground for the spring crops was far advanced and the open drills waiting.

This brings me to the ploughing, the start of the spring work, and there is a curious admission to be made. Though hardly any other operation was mechanised on our farms, most of the ploughing in the Glen, including the whole of ours the first spring, was done by a travelling tractor. This first season I was quite unable to plough and would have had to arrange for the work to be done in any case ; but nearly all of us gave much of the work to the tractor every year. During the critical few fine days of the West Highland spring there is more work waiting than can be crowded in. Autumn ploughing has been tried, but the general opinion is that in so wet a climate it encourages the leaching of the soil. Hence we were thankful to have the aid of the tractor with the ploughing. As a Fifeshire man put it to me, " The tractor's the boy to get the work done." But I was never resigned to this arrangement. The tractor, for good and for ill, was the representative of just that world which has been threatening to engulf the Highland values we had come to study.

As much as anybody I am fascinated by clever and powerful machines. To see a tractor plough in a day the ground that would have required most of a week from a man and a pair is an experience that gives one a great respect for the powers of machinery ; wherever some new contraption is at work I gape with the best. There seems to be no resisting the trend towards better, more efficient ways of getting things done. Nobody wants to walk when he could cycle, or to cycle when he could go by car, or to go by car if there is some quicker, easier alternative. A journey must be made, or a field ploughed, or a house built : what traveller, ploughman or builder but will take the easiest, quickest way ? And yet . . .

The objections to the tractor are on two levels. The first of these may well be dismissed as trivial : that we don't much like the tractor itself. It is not merely that a horse is a more interesting object than a machine, though it is a poor life that does not offer plenty of objects for affection, and nobody in his senses could be fond of a tractor. Nor is it the twisted, unhuman posture that a tractorman must adopt most of the day—for that matter a horse-ploughman is said to be recognisable from his stoop. It is rather that the clatter, smell and speed of the tractor dominate the field in which it is working. Gone are all the many small contacts with animal and vegetable life (Burns's " wee, sleekit, cowrin', tim'rous beastie " for instance, and his " wee, modest, crimson-tipped flower ") that give rise to so many momentary pleasures in farming. Life, after all, is a succession of moments no less than a succession of years.

If these are hardships, they are hardships that might be gladly endured for the sake of better food all round. The real objection to the tractor goes deeper. The tractor is one more bond subjecting a man to influences beyond his control.

A farmer who buys a tractor, like a country that allows its population to outgrow the number it can feed, is giving hostages to fortune. The tractor costs a lot of money, often borrowed money, and the work must therefore be arranged to suit the machine. " Keep the tractor moving." You cannot breed tractors on the farm, or grow your own paraffin. You must, whatever happens, sell something to pay off the cost of the tractor and to buy fuel. Britain as a whole must, whatever happens, sell something to purchase oil. The crofter's great asset is his relative independence ; the more machinery he buys the more closely is he enmeshed in a world of trade wars, world-wide devil-take-the-hindermost struggle, booms and slumps ; the more dependent is he upon people who never heard his name. A few of our neighbours did manage to do the whole of their own ploughing, but most of us were driven by the logic of the situation to make use of the hired tractor ; had we stayed long enough at Achbeg, D. and I might even have been driven by the same logic to purchase a two-wheeled light tractor ourselves ; the electric fence we did later put up was, after all, open to just the same objections on a smaller scale. But it is a line of development that leads straight out of the Highlands— not necessarily to the Gorbals, but at least to Birmingham, Pittsburgh and Dniepropetrovsk. Perhaps George Orwell's attitude is the most reasonable : " The machine has got to be accepted, but it is probably better to accept it rather as

one accepts a drug—that is, grudgingly and suspiciously.
Like a drug, the machine is useful, dangerous, and habit-
forming. The oftener one surrenders to it the tighter its
grip becomes."

In the short run, at least, the tractor has nearly all the
trumps. We were (as I have said) glad enough to accept
the help of Malcolm MacS., a crofter who lived " over the
hill " and kept a tractor and a lorry for work on contract.
He stayed for a few days in the Glen and in that short time
had all the ploughing finished.

Our first concern after ploughing was to sow the ley
corn (oats) on Achmore and Achbeg. First I gave the
ground a rub-over with the spike-harrows, to make sure
there were no cracks into which the seed could fall and be
lost. Care was needed at the headlands to prevent the spikes
from turning back the tough slices of turf. Donald followed, sowing. We did not use a seed drill, but broadcast
the seed so that it fell into the hollows of the furrows.
The depth of the seed is fairly uniform when sown thus,
though this is one of the jobs that a machine does a little
better as well as faster. Most of the crofters sow in the
age-old way, swinging the left arm and the right in time
with their striding. If a skilled man has done the work
it is hard to tell from the braided corn where he walked,
so even is the braid ; but not if a beginner has done the
work, or if a gusty wind at the time of sowing has carried
a double sowing to some parts and left ugly bare patches
in between. I tried my hand at broadcasting sulphate on
the Triangle later. The grass grew in ridges. The cattle
grazed the better grass and left the poorer. Rashes grew
where the cattle did not graze ; and I am afraid the mark
of my handiwork will be on that field until it is ploughed
again—if any tenant sees fit to take up again the losing
battle with the riverside rashes. For corn, both Donald
and I preferred an alternative device. The seed is tipped
into a bag carried on a band over the shoulder. Under
the bag there is a small circular pan with vanes, made to
rotate by the thong of a bow held in the right hand. This

ingenious contrivance is called a fiddle, and indeed the movement of the sower is precisely like that of a peasant fiddler holding his instrument in the old-fashioned way. I found that by choosing a still enough day, making careful calculations with the help of a spring balance, moving sticks across the field systematically as landmarks, and taking my time generally, I could achieve much the same result as anyone else ; but the crofters achieve it by striding over their fields with a seeming off-handedness and in half the time. Time is important when there are so few days dry enough and still enough for the work.

Once the corn-seed was in the ground the rest was just harrowing, and attempting to discourage the gulls, which always came in flocks. I believe they had some system of passing round the word—" Sowing at Achbeg to-day "— and all the gulls of Wester Ross came to the feast. A good tilth must be harrowed over the seed, first with the spikes, later the chains. Harrowing is said to be heavy on man and horse, but it is steady work that leaves plenty of attention over for the larks, the new green on the larches, and the comings and goings on the Glen road, and I always enjoyed it. Even on the occasion when, having sown the corn, we were caught by the weather, and I had to harrow away until the ground was like porridge, I still enjoyed it.

Of course, in harrowing and in the rest of the horse-work, I made all the blunders of the novice. As with any other job, there are countless important details to be learned from experience and from advice. I suppose that every beginner has to knock the hub-rim off a cart before he will realise how closely the horse's nose must graze the far post when turning in at a gateway, and to disentangle a spiky mass of harrows before getting the proper feel of the two reins at headlands. A cart can behave alarmingly on a steep brae. Owing to the amount of play between the shafts and the horse's sides (it usually increases as winter rations begin to " tell " on the horse), the cart tends to flap over to one side and mount the bank. I discovered this when we were going for firewood in Argyll. My attention was taken up by the difficulty of keeping the horse on his feet on a very steep rocky track. "Watch your cart," shouted my employer. And there it was, one wheel high on the bank, and looking as though it must somersault on to the horse or bounce into the drop beyond the bank. In some cases experience would be too costly a teacher. I was given much good advice at odd times, often backed by gruesome stories of the cost of neglect. William, in Argyll, warned me never to approach a horse at his feed without a loud "Steady, boy," and told me of a man kicked clean through his stable door by both hind hoofs of a mare who had never kicked before. I heard, too, of a horse found strangled having been tied in his stall by a rope not counterweighted, and of a man who, forgetting to glance at the heads of a pair of horses to see if they were quarrelling, stooped at the swingle-trees and had his skull cracked by a kick not meant for him at all. I think the most gruesome story was of a man in Patagonia. Some ways of holding a rein-rope are safe enough, but others are not : should the horse bolt, the tautness may lock the coil round the hand into a knot. The man in question was riding a horse with the rein crossed over his hand the wrong way. The horse bolted, threw him, and dragged him, with consequences better left undescribed.

There was little danger, however, from Dicky and Prince, but an incident occurred one morning that must have tried even Dicky's patience. Donald and I were, for once, making a really early start. We were going up the Glen to help sow the corn there. We greased the wheels of both carts, harnessed up, loaded on grubber, spike-harrows, chains, traces, and all the accessories, and started towards the gate. But we had somehow forgotten to replace one of the keys that keep on the wheels. There was a loud crack and a jolt ; one wheel had come off Dicky's cart. I have a vivid mental snapshot of the moment—the sun, just rising, glinting on the wet cobwebs, the cart at an astonishing angle, and Dicky glancing round over his right shoulder, waiting for further instructions.

When the ley corn was sown we started on the black-ground corn, and the procedure was much the same, with this difference. A week or ten days after the corn was in, we sowed grass-seed and gave it just the lightest harrowing with the chains. Some men preferred to brush it over with a bundle of faggots only—anything that would stir it in without breaking the shoots from the corn which had by now begun to germinate. Any weeds that were growing were given a final discouragement as well. If time permitted we rolled the ground in order to make a firm seed-bed and to press in stones that would otherwise give trouble to scythe and mower-blade later in the summer. Our roller was a home-made compound of wire, wood, stack-rope and iron bars, with a cart-axle, stones, alder-trunks and anything else for weight, all mounted on a workmanlike section of a pine-trunk. Nothing was quite rigid. Since the shafts could move through a fair angle without any effect upon the roller, there was an incalculable lag between stimulus and response. When in repose, the two shafts made a gaunt V-sign, one pointing at the zenith and the other at about 45 degrees ; when in action, the one knocked on the horse's right shin and the other tore straw from his collar behind the left ear. An eccentric pin gave the whole thing a limp. On level ground the operator sat on the logs, not for comfort (walking was less strenuous) but to add weight. I used to pile on sacks of stones for the same reason, but under the influence of the vibration they became completely amorphous and never stayed on for long. Eventually I found that the whimsies of the machine could be damped down and the horse more effectually linked to it if I superimposed the shafts of my cart on those of the roller with the help of many fathoms of stack-rope.

The roller had two merits. In spite of the intricacy of steering, it made a good job of the rolling : and it cost nothing whatever. It was just the thing for a croft.

The last and hardest part of the spring work was the preparation of the ground for the potatoes. A good tilth had to be prepared, first with the grubber and then with the harrows. The grubber, which has nine teeth mounted on springs so that they churn up the earth, is very heavy on the horses, and our hills made matters worse. We could seldom spare time for the tilth we should have liked, though we knew that lumpy potato-ground means difficult hoeing in the summer. The tilth once prepared, drills are opened up. This is difficult work. The first line is marked out with twigs, and the plough should catch them on the front of the sock as it opens the first drill. A spike dragging beside the plough scratches a line for the next drill, and so on. The process may sound easy, but a drill-plough is a tricky thing at all times. Moreover, if drills go over a brow or into a hollow, the drills tend to become wider or narrower and the later drills are cumulatively out of the true. All ploughmen take pride in the straightness of their line, and a well-drilled field is a great pleasure to look at.

Next, the dunging. Almost the whole midden goes out, and there are stiff backs before the work is done. Provided you are not racing against the clock, however, it is satisfying work. I never minded how late into the evening it went on, when I was working at my own speed. There is something stimulating in the odour of clean dung. We never troubled to wash our blackened fingers when tea and scones were brought out to us, but seemed to suffer no ill consequences.

Our steady pegging-away at the grubbing, drilling and dunging culminated in the day of planting. All our neighbours used to turn out to help one another on planting days, and one or two of them were persuaded to have a drill of their own in our field or Donald's—poor thanks, but the best we could offer. With graips or hay-forks we worked along the drills, spreading the little heaps of dung. Sowing the artificial usually fell to my lot. If the day is windy the gritty mixture goes into your eyes and down your collar, and makes your hair impossible to comb. Some of the seed potatoes would be medium-sized tubers, the rest larger tubers cut in advance by the women-folk in the windy barn. Usually there were two kinds of seed—one or two bags of new seed, which would provide the bulk of next year's seed, and the second-year seed. We kept to Kerr's Pinks, which cropped well, though Donald grew also Golden Wonders (highly esteemed by the Highlanders, who are very particular about their potatoes), Edsall Blues and other varieties. With complications of ownership, variety and age there was plenty of opportunity for argument, and the good-humour of communal work lightened the task, as always. It was on the potato-field that Teena made a remark that still pleases me for its complete good-humour and detachment. Teena was much teased on the field because she was past twenty-one but still unmarried. The conversation this day turned upon some much-married public figure. From a distance I heard Teena's voice, in an accent that many mistook for Irish :

"Isn't it strange, now, that some can get six when others can get none at all ! "

Children, too, helped to the limit of their ability : the sense of responsibility of children brought up on a croft is very noticeable to the in-comer. By tea-time all the planting would be finished and Donald would be splitting the drills, so as to bury dung and tubers alike. This, too, is difficult and heavy work. One horse must walk on the drill all the time. Having been obliged for weeks past to keep strictly to the hollow, he now finds himself expected to keep to the ridge (to prevent trampling on the potatoes). All of the tubers must be covered over by nightfall, in case of frost or heavy rain, though in emergency it was enough to split only alternate drills that day. When all else was finished, and nothing more could be done, we all left Donald splitting the drills of the last potato-field of the year, and went in to supper at Achmore. We supped, and talked, and night fell, and a thin paring of moon shone, and still there was no sound of the horses. I went to meet

Donald on the road, and soon heard the jingle of harness approaching.

" I can't think what the drills will look like in daylight," he said ; " towards the end I had only the moon to guide me. There is frost already—I had to get them covered at all costs."

But they looked well enough next morning, and the splitting of the remaining drills straightened out any imperfections.

The work on turnips or kale, when we managed to sow any, was almost entirely the same as that on the potatoes. With it the cycle of the field-work, like that of the sheep-work, has come full circle, and we are ready again for hoeing, haymaking, harvesting, tatty-hooking, and—the winter.

CHAPTER X

" Under the cow hangs the milk. It is arranged for milking. When people milk the milk comes, and there is never an end to the supply. How the cow does it I have not yet realised, but it makes more and more."—Scottish school-child, quoted in a London newspaper.

Though our second and third years naturally followed the general seasonal rhythm of the first, there was plenty of variety in the work and in the conditions. On one day we might be burning heather high up in the hills, and on another fencing down in the bog; at one time breaking ice for the cattle to drink and at another searching for them as they cowered from the midges down in the rashes.

The flies and midges were a pest in summer. The cows would sink into egg-shaped nests among the rashes in order to offer the smallest possible area of skin, and rely upon a flickering tail for protection from above. On the worst days we kept them in altogether. When I had occasion to milk Jean in the open one evening, the midges caught in the jets formed almost a scum on the milk.

There were plenty of interesting or amusing incidents. One winter afternoon I shut most of the hens in the byre by inadvertence, and when later I went along with my lantern to milk, the place was like a taxidermist's, with somnolent hens perched everywhere—on the hay-racks, the rafters, the stalls and even the cows themselves. For a week in the summer the midnight hush was broken by pitiful squawks from the pullets—now much too big for the coop in which they insisted upon cramming themselves although their former broody had long forsaken it—while we transferred them to more permanent quarters. (Later we solved this problem by shifting the coop a yard a day until it was inside the hen-house; but if we moved the coop too far at once the miserable birds huddled on the spot where they considered their home ought to be.) An otter ambled by within a few yards of me when I was working on a fence; he took not the slightest notice of me or of Nell. Nell watched with interest and glanced up at me for instructions. On another occasion I was eating my sandwiches on Ree Breac, ensconced in the heather for protection from the wind, when a herd of deer came bounding towards me from behind some rising ground. They caught my scent and in a small fraction of a second all that movement was locked in absolute stillness. Nothing moved as they stared up-wind. Then just as suddenly they were in full movement again down-wind, and I watched them lightly bounding to the horizon, apparently oblivious of all the slopes and the inequalities of ground.

There were also more serious occasions. Just at bed-time one wild March night, word went round to all the men in the Glen that someone was adrift in a boat off Fernaig shore. The hurried 'phone message was not clear, but it seemed that a man had gone out in a rowing-boat to strengthen the moorings of a skiff at anchor off Plockton and had been carried away by the wind, which was driving straight across to us from Plockton. A rowing-boat could never ride the white-topped waves that were beating on the shore, and there were cruel rocky islands at many points in the turmoil. We patrolled the beach just beyond reach of the clutching waves, and peered into the darkness. Lights of other watchers twinkled from Ardneaskan and all round the bay, but we could make out little except one or two rollers coming in, and the dim shapes of the nearer islands. At any moment a man's life might depend upon instantaneous action. All ended happily. A light was seen to be flashing from a point beyond the old light-house, and its position remained unchanged. We heard at length that the skiff itself had dragged its anchor. It could ride the waves easily enough so long as it kept clear of the rocks. By good fortune the anchor held again before the expected disaster, and during a lull the man was taken off by another boat. Grim relics sometimes floated in from the Atlantic to remind us that in the bigger struggle that had not yet ended, fate was not always so kind.

Our work ignored the clock if not the calendar. When the outside world put its clocks on, " interfering with God's hours that always were from the time of the Creation " as one old friend put it, we were as likely to put our own back, in effect, because much crop-work cannot be started till the dew has lifted. If we wanted to go to a Red Cross Sale in Kyle or an Agricultural Show at Conchra, we had but to arrange the work accordingly ; and on Sundays only the minimum of routine animal work was ever done.

Much has been said against the Highland Sunday, but we came to believe that even on purely secular grounds there was a balance of argument in its favour. One day of absolute peace for rest and contemplation was assured. In theory each individual could give himself a rest one day in seven, but when work is so pressing there would be too much waste of nervous energy in making and adhering to the decision. The purpose of a social convention is to save just that waste, and to prevent mutual interference. A farmer in Lewis—like ourselves, a foreigner —saved his hay on a Sunday that happened to be the only fine day in weeks. He was visited by a protesting deputation of Ministers and others, to the indignation of the journalists ; but having experienced the English Sunday, which is in some places rather less peaceful than any of the other days, we felt that on the whole the Ministers were in the right. He was starting to undermine a tradition that involved far more than the fate of a particular crop of hay. When the equinoctial gales demolished our haystack on a Sunday, or when sheep were struck by maggot, then there was little choice but to make good the damage ; but routine field-work was never undertaken or even contemplated.

At the other extreme a start at 4.30 a.m. for the early

Portachullin from Achbeg. This hill was the common grazing of the Portachullin crofters.

Hens. They cannot forage for themselves in snowy weather.

The Glen under snow. Miss Stewart's croft in the centre. The alders along the Ascaig stand out more sharply.

Meallan under snow. The Pleiades appeared to glide straight out of the cone at the summit.

train might be necessary several days in succession, and one night we had just two hours in bed. The seasonal work often kept us out late. We harrowed the newly-sown corn one evening until the pied wagtails that always follow the harrows were mere half-discerned flecks ; we whispered to the horses in order not to wake our neighbours, and when we finished I could not find my jacket in the darkness. Quite often, when we thought we were finished, a cow would prove to be bulling, or the ducks would still be foraging somewhere out on the Hill. (To leave them out would mean no eggs in the morning, and if the fox were around no ducks.) Very late one night a cow of Donald's was reported to be in the bog and we all hurried off with ropes and planks. Voices echoed against the alders in the still air, until a loud splashing told us that the cow was now free and being driven down the river-bed. The full moon glided up above the conifers. We talked on the road home, in no hurry to go in from the cool, scented night air.

Not that the work was excessive, at least for the men-folk ; though for the womenfolk I am not so certain. They had all the toil of running a home and the worry of feeding a multitude of helpers—in face of short rations—at an hour or two's notice, and much of the burden of the seasonal and routine work to carry also. We heard a story of a crofter who, when asked if he thought of marrying, unguardedly replied, " If I don't get married, I'll have to get a horse." For any woman whose heart was in it and who had the physical stamina, it was, I believe, as good a life as any in the world, but the strain tells on some. This was one of the considerations that influenced us (or rather me) in the decision to leave when the war ended. Other more private considerations do not concern this narrative.

Our main cash income continued to be derived from the sheep and the cattle. Although maggot was never again quite as bad as in the first season, it continued to be a serious threat, and it was reported that some calves

L

and even a pony had been struck. After the experience of hunting for sheep in Strome Wood, I had asked the Forestry people to restore the burnt march fence on the top, but this only created a new problem. It meant that when sheep did get in, it was harder than ever to get them out. And they were constantly in—partly because the gate was so often left open, but partly because the Achbeg sheep were no sheep to let a few strands of wire stand between them and good grazing. They were, I believe, wilder than those of any nearby farm. On the highest and rockiest hills there are sheep that may not be handled once in a year. At the mere whiff of a man or a dog they are off at great speed, and to add to the dog's perplexity they sometimes scatter instead of bunching. It would be almost as easy to gather deer. Our sheep were quieter than these, but for several generations they had been accustomed to broken walls and weak fences, they had learned that stolen grazing is often the sweetest, and they had come to regard fences as a hint or a challenge, according to the mood of the moment, but never as a barrier. When they were bent on wandering there was not a ditch, wall, six-wire-fence, or even deer-fence in the district but they would eventually find a way over, under, through or (failing all else) round it.

When we were dipping at Braientra fank, a ewe of ours, having leaped several walls, stood at a distance, obviously uncertain whether her loneliness was too high a price to pay for her freedom. After she had watched the flock beyond the high wire fence for some minutes, gregariousness prevailed. She walked a few steps, broke into a slow run, and gathered speed. Everyone stopped work to watch, as she was making straight for an almost impossible fence and anything might happen. Without a sign of faltering she took the fence cleanly in her stride. " Like a roe-deer," said somebody, " just like any roe-deer."

Later on, at a time when I had no dog, I found some old cast ewes and some gimmers astray on the Lower Flat. They were meant to be in a park—the gimmers beyond reach of the tup, and the ewes ready for trucking when needed. I doubt if there was better grass in the West of Scotland than the Aberystwith ley (of which more later), and well they knew it when I was trying to keep them out : but now that they were being kept *in*, the dry autumn heather of the Flat (as palatable, one would think, as wood shavings) seemed to have become irresistible. I edged them on to the road and towards the Falls, planning an elaborate strategy in which I figured as dog and master by turns. However, Blackie, who was the ringleader, unknowingly helped me out. She led them single file to the fence at the top of the bank. Here they all paused and looked round at me. I gave them every encouragement. Blackie ducked her head, both horns of which had been lost by now on just such occasions, pushed it under the bottom wire, and began to wriggle. It was literally uphill work, and the wire was reasonably tight and close to the ground. Inch by inch she wriggled away until she shot out like a cork at the other side. The others followed. A spindle of wool on the wire, with Blackie's coarser fibres showing amongst the softer Cheviot staple, marked the spot for future convenience. Half a dozen times in the next few days the same thing happened until it settled down to a routine. Perhaps it was wrong of me to condone the misdemeanour, but I had little choice. Scraping under wires, though bad for ewes near to lambing, does less harm in the autumn, and the old ewes were soon to be graded anyway. The gimmers, with their lives before them, had picked up Blackie's evil ways, just as Blackie herself at some distant time must have taken lessons from a wily black-faced scoundrel of a mother ; but since she was teaching them how to get out of the field for her own good, I felt she could teach them the way back in for mine.

If the lower wires were loose or staples missing, the sheep preferred to go through the fences rather than over or under. However often I brought hammer and wire-strainer to the job, they always beat me in a day or two.

Only once did I see sheep pass between the upper wires. A group had leaped over the fence into the Triangle and they were enjoying the clover that was meant to be reserved for hay. I sent Nell round them and they bolted to leave as they had entered. The slope, however, made the outward leap impossible ; the leader simply bounced back off the wire. My intention was to take them to the gate, but they were determined to leave in their own way. They tried the lower wires and found them too close and taut. Then the leader quite deliberately walked backwards a few steps, paused, and took a running leap towards the wider space at the top. She stream-lined herself in mid-air like a swallow and came to rest half-way through, stuck tight. Ten seconds of violent convulsions and she was through. One other ewe followed in the same fashion, but the older ones preferred after all to submit to Nell's guidance.

As for going round the fences, they made a practice in dry weather of walking along the river-bed and into an adjoining park. There were meant to be barriers carrying the lines of the fences across the river, but in dry weather the river-bed became almost a highway. It was humiliating to watch sheep taking a short cut across the arable, for all the world as though there were no fences at all. And one bunch of sheep learned to make a detour across Portachullin ground into Strome Wood when the main fence became a little difficult.

It may be imagined, therefore, what difficulty we had chasing sheep in Strome Wood once the march fence had been sealed, and on a number of occasions we had " the squad " to help us drive the wood. A lamb broke its leg in one of these hunts. We devised splints and the bone set remarkably well, though at a slight angle. This particular lamb never learned caution, and travelled at an astonishing speed on three legs until the fourth had mended.

In our third summer we tried a different method of defeating maggot. Donald had, as has been said, burnt a large tract of ground up on Ree Breac, at a height to which the blow-fly does not seem to rise. On three sides the ground was encircled by the upper Forestry deer-fence, though it was open on the fourth. We mixed our flocks and drove them up to this higher grazing as soon as maggot seriously threatened. The stratagem worked very well. Only one ewe, which was struck before being taken up, suffered from maggot. Watching and gathering the sheep over so vast a tract, and driving them down for clipping and dipping and up again, took much time and effort, especially as Donald's sheep (being newly bought in) tended to wander eastwards—towards the open end of the horse-shoe fence. Our own gravitated towards their own ground, where the deer-fence gave them plenty to think about. Any that got through would eventually filter back on to our own ground.

Our sheep-work on the high ground was especially pleasant while the heather was in bloom. Donald's quickness in discovering white heather astonished me—I never found a single sprig. I understand, however, that those who sell white heather to exiles in the big towns are saved much labour by the bleaching powers of ammonia.

During the last months of our stay at Achbeg, I was entirely dependent in the sheep-work on help from Donald and his dog Prince, for we lost poor Nell. Distemper swept through the district, killing many of the best dogs. Nell appeared to recover and begged to be allowed to come with me on the hill. I made the mistake of letting her come too soon. She relapsed, and although D. stayed up night after night trying to save her, she eventually died. We did not succeed in obtaining another.

The reduction in the losses from maggot was partly due, no doubt, to a change in the weather. When we grumbled at the weather, as we did, endlessly, the older people always maintained that in their youth the winters had been far more wintry and the summers had been genuine summers. Despite my doubts, in the middle of our stay at Achbeg the weather reverted to this earlier pattern. Snow and frost caught us in early November, before we had lifted the potatoes or dipped the sheep.

Luckily a respite enabled us to rush the potatoes into clamps and sheds, and we dipped the sheep on a day that threatened to be followed by a night of heavy frost. Donald and I kept ours in sheds overnight, or I believe they would have been rigid by morning.

Then the real winter began. Snow fell to a level depth of a couple of feet. We awoke in the mornings to find snowdrifts in the house wherever there were normally draughts. A caller, snatching his hat too suddenly from his head, pulled out tufts of hair. Soon the Hill and the Flat were wholly encased in ice-covered snow. In former times the flocks included strong wedders who could scrape down to the heather-shoots, but none of our sheep could penetrate this crust. They took to racing about the Hill in ravenous packs, searching for moss and dried grass wherever vertical rock-surfaces broke through the snow. Nothing but thirst and hunger would bring the hens out of their shed, and at most they scuttled across to the warmth of the byre. Throughout this spell the byre was the one warm place. In cleaning out the stable I had to chip the bedding away from the floor, but not so the byre. A portcullis of icicles gently dropped from the eaves as the warmth of the cows melted the snow above them. The ducks, more venturesome than the hens, made short rapid journeys over the snow and then plopped down suddenly, tucking in all their extremities, until they felt warm enough for the next dash. No quantity of piled bedding seemed to keep the frost out of the potatoes in the barn ; and when Isabella ran completely out of coal we took a bag along the shore to her on a contrived horse-sledge. There stood the herons, fishing on one leg, as though it were the height of summer. Prince and the cows were eating their way through the hay at almost double the normal rate, and we resigned ourselves to the need for buying in baled hay later—a costly business, but less costly than trying to sell cattle in such weather. We were at any rate luckier than some of the higher farms which had to have hay dropped from aeroplanes.

Our chief worry was the sheep. As the weeks went by and they came nearer to lambing, they grew thinner and weaker until many were staggering. We put out hay, but few would touch it after a day or two. One ewe died. Donald and I at length decided that if the thaw did not come within two days we should follow the plan of a Welsh farmer who drove a snow-plough over parts of his ground and saved most of his sheep where neighbours lost their flocks. The thaw did come. A puff of warm air drifted in from somewhere, and by morning the rivers were in flood. Plates of ice jostled against the keystone of Achmore bridge and swept away all the river barriers. Along the railway line the water rose to the door-handles of the platform buildings, and chained cattle were released from byres with the greatest difficulty. Fortunately the floods had abated before the lambs were born, or many would have been drowned in the hillside torrents. But the weather had yet one more trick to play. In the midst of lambing came the blackthorn winter, or " gab o' May," with wind and heavy frost. At dusk one particularly bitter evening, D. and I went to the Hill and gathered in all the lambs we could find in the failing light. They were snug enough in the barn, but one that stayed on the hill with its mother was dead by morning. It says much for the hardiness of hill-sheep that they were none the worse for their winter trials. When the grass " came " the ewes settled down to building up both themselves and their lambs, and the drop in lamb prices next autumn reflected not the condition of the lambs but some freak of market conditions.

There followed a summer that made up for the trials of the winter ; our anxiety was no longer the rain but the drought. Haymaking was a pleasure now and though we ourselves never trusted the continuance of the fine weather enough to abandon our pyramids, there is no doubt that this year Donald's system brought the better results. Our third winter, that of 1945-46, was milder, but the general improvement in the summer weather continued to help us in the rush of our final spring-work and the preparations for departure.

The cattle work too followed much the same course as in the first year. The cows we bought in at different times proved all to have their own personality. Jean was too fat. However much I cut down her ration she continued to thrive, until I discovered that she systematically stole whatever she could reach of her neighbour's food before touching her own. Her long grasping tongue would pull one strand through any small hole in the partitions and a continuous rope of hay or straw was made to follow. Polly, a bony black animal, was too stupid to know that a doorway is for going through, and Marie would not " let down " until she had been given some tit-bit—a fault we tried to overcome by slowly diminishing the tit-bit.

Marie was our last purchase. Milk had fallen off badly during our third winter because Carrie had failed to calve at the allotted time. Winter-calving cows are expensive to buy, but we reckoned that the increased milk sales would more than off-set the drop in value that we must expect at our waygoing. We heard of a good cow some miles along the railway-line, at a very lonely spot, and the day I spent going over to see her was typical of many. Along the railway banks, the younger green spikes of the bracken had trailing below them bunches of the dead brown growth of previous years, a perpetual *memento mori*; and a jagged criss-cross of snow picked out the gulleys and strata of Applecross beyond the water. As I passed the mouth of the Glen I had a glimpse of smoke from our own chimney. My thoughts ran largely on prices—I was checking the offer I could make on the cow—but not to the exclusion of the reproachful " coo " of the eider drakes out on the loch, or the more incisive cry of the oyster-catchers, or the friendly company of an old heron who kept settling a little ahead of me but never allowed me to come too close.

Emerging from one of the gorge-like railway cuttings, I heard a gruff voice among the trees high above me, obviously addressed to a dog. It was Jimmy McH., who had worked much on the railways and had a great store of tales of dynamite and whisky. He was urging along a heavy Cheviot ewe. Jimmy, though active for his years, was no longer young enough to be wrestling with a stubborn ewe on such a slope, and I went up to lend a hand. Jimmy told me that this ewe of his had always lived on the ledges of the crag that reached nearly a thousand feet into the air behind us. She had brought up her lamb there and had lived almost independently of her owner. Jimmy had been trying to get her down, but when cornered she had leaped from a rock, grazing and bruising herself, but breaking no bones. Now Jimmy was trying to urge her up to the road and thence along to his croft. He helped me to get her on my shoulders, and very slowly I made my way up to the road. Blood from a cut artery spattered over my jersey and breeches, but luckily my smartening-up for this expedition had been perfunctory. The road reached, we put her on her four feet, but she refused to move for a while. Experiment showed that the best way to get her along was for me to waddle behind her with my fingers deeply clawed into the wool of her rump. She would run for twenty yards, when my one difficulty was to restrain her, and then stop as though she had hit a wall, when the difficulty was to avoid pitching clean over her. A period of rigid immobility would end as suddenly as it had begun. In this erratic manner the poor beast was propelled at length to the little dip where stood Jimmy's house. Seldom if ever have I travelled a more laborious half-mile. But the sheep was now home, where she would receive all attention if she could be saved, and where a use would still be found for her if she could not.

I returned to my journey, which took me now through rhododendrons, beeches, and huge conifers of many strange kinds, some of them bunched like celery and others a single swaying column. A dead millionaire had chosen this innocent form of ostentation. But there is no bribing Time.

Drifts of beech leaves and fallen boughs now lay undisturbed.

Arrived at the lonely house, I was given tea at a window
that looked across the water to the contrasting sociability
of Plockton, and then we went up to see the cow Marie.
I liked her. She should give a good blocky calf, and yet
milk reasonably well. We haggled without a decision but
I promised to write, and I set off on the return journey.
I did write and we came to terms. A week later I again
set out, this time in stinging rain, had tea at the window
by the loch, confirmed the bargain, and started out with
Marie on a halter. She led well, except that she delighted
in edging me into the drenched roadside bushes. Gorse
flowers sparkled bravely in the gathering dark before we
reached home, where the cows were waiting angrily at the
gate (for D. was away in Edinburgh). I suppose I should
have added two days' labour to her cost on the books,
but these two journeys—like that to the bull at Ardelve,
already described—and many others, I should not willingly
have missed.

Marie calved on Christmas Eve, a few days later. I
kept running over from a Township meeting to see that
all was well, and Gordon helped me when the crisis came,
before hurrying home to play Father Christmas to his own
children.

As soon as the weather permitted I put her out in a
field with the other cows and with Prince. She challenged
the cows one by one and then discovered Prince. Possibly
she had never seen a horse before. She sniffed him over
from head to tail and worked down to his hind hoofs.
I watched anxiously from the rock, but to Prince she was
just one more cow and he never kicked. When I last
looked back, Marie was staring incredulously at the electric
fence.

This last was an experiment that we decided to try,
partly in the interests of the cattle and partly in the interests of the crops, particularly the grass. We grazed
every available corner of grass, sometimes tethering Ruby

on our own or Miss MacL.'s lawn. (Ruby could pass
through the gateway easily enough when hungry, but
scraped the posts on both sides when coming out.) We
found this inadvisable after a while, however, not so much
because of what she took away as because of what she left
behind. There are many patches of grass on a farm which
could be producing milk, but which lose most of their
value before the crops are lifted and the cattle can be turned
on to them. In order to keep to a rotation on a croft,
fields must often be temporarily subdivided. Ordinary
fencing is much too expensive and takes much too long
to erect where the barrier will need to be removed in a
year or two. Electric fencing works on a different prin-
ciple ; in place of what may be called siege tactics it
employs psychological tactics. A single strand of wire is
run along on insulators at nose height, and connected to
a special shocking coil that sends harmless but quite
startling pulses along its whole length about once a second.
This "unit" we fitted for greater safety in the byre where
it tick-tocked contentedly in a dark corner like a grandfather clock, to the occasional astonishment of visitors.
The animals, once they have experienced the full shock,
keep clear of the wire. Their attitude is one of respect
rather than fear, for the grass cropped short extends right
up to the fence and a little beyond—just as far as a neck
will safely reach. Cheetah, indeed, at once discovered that
by going down on her knees she could reach a little farther,
and was often to be seen in that inelegant posture enjoying
a strip of grass that was entirely her own. A light wire
carried by light posts at intervals of a dozen yards or so
will usually restrain the cow (there is one on every farm)
who batters a way through or over all more conventional
barriers. Once the cows have tried the wire the current
can be switched off for a fortnight or so, when they begin
to become inquisitive again.

We reckoned, then, that an electric fence would enable
us to make better use of our ground, and in particular to
be systematic about the grazing. It is far better, by all

accounts, to graze each patch hard in turn, and then to rest it, than to let the cattle take a bite wherever and whenever they can find it. The individual grass plants have a better chance to establish themselves, the balance of species is preserved longer, the patchiness of grazing is at any rate reduced, and the proportion of leaf to stem is increased. We also reckoned that we should save a good deal of time on our scattered farm. It is quite easy to spend an hour a day driving the milk cows at their own pace to and from the farther parks. We planned to run the wire so that it formed a lane to our farther fields, with gates that could be set to lead to any one of them, and overhead loops above any open gates. Then we could put the cows into the lane and leave the rest to them.

The apparatus arrived, and one drenching morning we rigged up a stretch of wire across the Wee Park by the steading for training the animals ; we put them all through the gate, and took shelter in the barn to watch through the slats. Maundy was the first to approach, and to our consternation she grazed her way under it without a twitch, soaking though she was. On the return journey she noticed the wire, investigated it in the manner proper to animals and recoiled violently. They all had their own reactions. Ruby was definitely offended, and Cheetah licked her hoofs in bewilderment. Prince snorted and galloped around in the rashes, sending up a spray of rain-drops. Two or three sniffs apiece were all that were needed to train them. We put all the animals on one side of the wire and some sheaves on the other, and went in for dinner.

We did not share the fears of Angus McG., who had seen the effects of a more serious electric shock, and predicted that our fence would kill every man and beast in the place, but we thought it well to warn the school-children ; I would go over to the school-house after dinner. When we came out, however, most of the children were already leaning over the dyke in uproarious enjoyment of a new game, the winner being he (or she) who could hold on longest. But the corn lay untouched by the cows.

Within its limitations the fence was both a convenience and an economy ; we had practically no trouble from loose contacts, short-circuiting due to weeds, or the unit itself, but there are two limitations that are—naturally—not stressed by the makers, which should be thought over by anyone about to try out the device.

First, the posts must be fairly strong. It is quite true, as the makers say, that cows will not press against the wire ; what they do not add is that the proximity of the wire will not deter the cows from rubbing every accessible part of their hides against the posts. Any cow revels in a good scratch. She puts every ounce of her weight into it, and she weighs about half a ton. We made the mistake of supposing that any bit of stick that would carry the wire would do, and had a good deal of trouble at first from grounded wires in consequence. A broken post not only makes a gap in the defences ; it dislocates the whole circuit.

Second, the fence is entirely useless against untrained animals. The just walk under, as Maundy did at the first approach, or drag it down. Hence any foreign cattle must be trained before they can be put into the wired parks ; and one's own cattle must be periodically reminded, even during the winter, when the fence is less needed—otherwise the wire is just a tangle by spring. There was, we heard, a long stretch of electric fencing in use as a deer-fence not far away, but from my slight knowledge of deer and my experience of the fencing, I believe that the warning notice without the wire would have had as much effect.

On the other hand, trained stock can readily be bluffed. When there was anything (a corn-stack, for example) that needed protection where there was no convenient source of shock, we looped a wire round with a good display of insulators and nothing else. The fraud was never detected.

It is said that in America, where electric fences are more widely used, some cattle come to pay no attention to the wire, while others pay so much that they will not approach any wire at all and are thus a great nuisance at market. We had no trace of either trouble.

Some of our calves we sold and others we kept, according to the milk requirements of the moment. The decision was always something of a gamble. In the autumn of our second year, calves were fetching more at three-quarters of a year than equivalent stirks a year older. In other words, farmers that year had put twelve months' food and labour into their stirks for less than nothing, and this in spite of relative war-time stability. What farming was like during the period of open world competition, when calves might bring in less than their freight and lambs less than rabbits, is best left to the imagination of the supporters of open world competition, if any remain.

One of our great difficulties was to anticipate the times of calving closely enough. I should be ashamed to say just how many of our calves were born out in the snow, in the far-off parks, and anywhere but in a calving pen. We always called in neighbours to confirm our judgment, and it seemed that a cow had only to hear the pronouncement, " No, she'll not calve to-day in any case," to go off in search of a quiet corner. In the end, I used to watch the cows almost continuously, and on crucial nights made myself a bed of sheaves in the byre. I was surprised to hear the moans, snorts, sneezes, yawns and other noises that go on all night in a byre ; Cheetah, whose weight was equal to that of six heavyweight boxers, was given to snoring.

The various out-door calvings went off smoothly enough ; but if the calf has once sucked, the cow may prove very difficult to milk. From the Face one Sunday, when I was up after a sick sheep, I saw an odd procession in the River Park ; D. with a neighbour's help, was trying to get Maundy and a tiny black calf along to the byre, whilst keeping them apart. We had hoped to make a milker of Maundy at the second lactation, and many fruitless hours did I spend pumping away at her. We had to give her her calf. With Ruby too we had difficulty, though for a different reason. During the weeks before calving she had become interested in a calf penned within sight of her, and she too refused to be a milker. She accepted her own calf Seppie willingly enough, but we had great difficulty in putting Walker, the other calf, on to her as well. She pushed him away brusquely whenever he approached. Walker found, however, that by hiding behind Seppie he could make a safe approach, and in this curious way the two calves always fed. Ruby became very protective, approaching all dogs and intruders of any kind with her horns down. When a hen, just as motherly over her thirteen chicks, strayed into the field, the strangest encounter took place, without a clear decision.

Our cattle were not TB tested, but tuberculosis is rare in animals kept in Highland conditions. Prairie cattle are almost entirely immune, whereas cattle intensively reared in large herds, forced to early maturity for milk or meat, and housed indoors, are prone to infection.

We were spared trouble from redwater, which is a danger in tick-infested areas, though we had to cope at different times with ringworm, warbles, and worst of all, mastitis. Ruby went as hard as a board in one of her quarters, and then Maundy too. We called in the vet, who confirmed that a streptococcus was the cause. He gave us sulphonamide drenches, and every eight hours for several days I had a tussle with the two cows, pouring fluid down their throats from a beer-bottle. It was, as usual, Donald who showed me how. The symptoms cleared up for a while, but we had always thenceforth to keep these two cows at one end of the byre, so that the milker's hands never passed from them to other cows.

Mastitis is one of the chief sources of loss to dairy farmers. If I were the Prince of Darkness, and in league with the various germs that cause mastitis, I should secure the following conditions :

(1) I should arrange for cows from a wide area to be concentrated in a single building.

(2) I should arrange for them to include a high pro-portion of infected beasts.

(3) I should cause the udder, teats and milk veins of each cow to be felt carefully by many hands that would then pass on unwashed to others.

(4) I should shuffle the cows and scatter them over the district again.

(5) I should cause the presence of latent disease to be kept secret so that the hands of unsuspecting milkers might continue to pass from infected to uninfected udders.

In this way I should hope to spread the germs to the greatest possible number of herds, and to affect the largest possible number of cows in each herd.

But if I visited a cattle market I should see that there was no need for me to do anything at all about it. Even the second requirement is fulfilled : the cows (like the coins) that circulate are the faulty ones, the others being treasured up in the herd.

In the end we decided to grade Maundy along with Cheetah. I took them and several animals belonging to our neighbours in to Dingwall, where they were joined by a Highland bull with the most impressive horns I have seen on any bull. Though he was as gentle as a lamb, the mere look of him cleared the street before us, and some Aristophanic comments were shouted from doorways. When later in the day I saw a group of beasts being driven at the double towards the railway-station and the slaughterhouse, with Maundy at their head, I felt that I had betrayed the trust of years. A number of us were working in the fields a few days later, and I was told that the week's meat ration had never been known to be so tough as that week.

As the time for our departure approached, our various animals departed in ones and twos. It was Prima, our first calf, herself now near to calving, that we gave up with the greatest reluctance. She was bought by a family who would, we knew, be good to her. Not until Mrs.

Carting coal. Oaks and a hedge of beech and hawthorn down towards the shore.

Across the Glen. View over Loch Carron to the hills nicknamed "Gladstone's Face."

The railway. It spans the sea end of the Glen, passes the raised beach, and cuts short the Portachullin strips.

Sawing wood. Oak, birch and alder are burned to eke out the coal.

McH. arrived with a halter to lead her away did it occur to me that I had never broken her to the halter. We attached a very long halter and let loose her byre-chain. A great tussle ensued in which I was dragged all round the steading and the garden, like a towed target. Each morning for the next week I exercised her on the halter, and when the McH.'s called again she behaved perfectly. She gave satisfaction, and the McH.'s sent a pat of her butter to us in England when she calved.

In our arrangements for departure and throughout our tenancy we found the Forestry Commission most accommodating landlords, but they were unpopular in the district. We had many conversations on this and other subjects at different times ; one, I remember, began, when a number of us were standing miserably in the rain, with the inconsequential remark, " They tell me the King gets a thousand pounds a day." The rights and wrongs of poaching often came up. The Highlanders have never accepted the laws which transferred to irresponsible visitors the rights that had always belonged to the people, and I learned some promising secrets which it would obviously be impossible to record here.

There are three other much-discussed topics on which, since there is no space to say much (even if I were competent to do so) and it would be misleading to say a little, it is wiser to say nothing at all ; they are Scottish nationalism, Scottish religion and Scottish education.

M

CHAPTER XI

"One soweth and another reapeth."—"St. John."

Dicky and Prince continued to work together on the ploughing, harrowing, drilling, harvesting and other field work of the two farms and some of the crofts. Apart from the ancient mower, practically nothing was communally owned, but amongst most of us there was free lending and borrowing. Each family saw to its own routine work, but as soon as any job required more hands, and at any time of crisis such as a flitting or an illness, there was spontaneous co-operation. Thus we had many of the advantages of communal effort, and yet each of us had his individual stake. Any attempt to collectivise the Glen would be resisted to the last ditch. We often discussed the Co-ops. Their activities in squeezing-out small traders were almost universally resented, yet their sales continued to mount. In point of fact the objections raised applied to all chain-stores, but the S.C.W.S. is the only one active on any scale on the West.

A holiday was given to paid workers to celebrate the victory in Europe and two of them chose to spend it helping Donald and me to put out the dung on his potato-field. With widespread famine threatening to continue for years to come, it seemed to me the only tolerable form of celebration. At times like potato-planting or harvest there was the same good-humoured crowd of neighbours on the field as before ; even the travelling bull-dozer driver, who probably didn't know my name, came and helped with our corn. It was on the cornfield that I first heard the story the Scots like to tell against themselves. It concerns an old Highlander who was cycling home with a hip flask in his pocket. He fell off the bicycle and, feeling something trickling down his side, was heard to mutter, " I hope it's blood."

Our horses were sometimes lent or hired to places farther afield, and on such an occasion Dicky has lately found his way into the national headlines. He was borrowed by a crofter on the far side of Loch Carron, which is 800 yards wide at the ferry, and fully double that for most of its length, and which has a powerful tidal current. He repeatedly broke out of the enclosures and tried to gain admittance to the ferry, where he was always turned back. Then he appeared, soaking wet, at the kitchen door of Achmore. Nobody had seen him in the water or on the beach, but he had certainly crossed by swimming. Dicky's years were beginning to tell on him towards the end of our stay. We sold Prince to Donald on our departure ; thus Prince found a home to our liking, and Dicky could go into partial retirement.

Donald used sometimes to do the horse-work on the strips at Portachullin (the only crofts, in the strict sense of the word, in the Glen). The railway embankment has been driven over the ancient strips, leaving patches many of which are impossibly small. Some, I am sure, were no bigger than the carpets in many a public building. The horses would soon be reeling with the constant turning ; and I calculated that the headlands made up just a third of one of the strips. Farther along there were strips that were more workable, though the horses sank from view half-way along, where the steeper slope down to the shore began, and they turned actually on the seaweed and shingle. Some of the best grass in the district grew on these strips. Only four houses now stand by the shore and there are no children at all ; within living memory there were over a dozen families.

Although most of our ploughing was done by the tractor, I learned to do horse-ploughing of a rough kind. My first attempts were made on the strip of black-ground from which the first year's potatoes had been lifted. Black-ground ploughing is the easiest, partly because the more catastrophic inequalities can be levelled off later with the harrows whereas ley-ploughing, to be tolerable at all, must lie in even pleats. (Nevertheless I have sometimes seen ley-ploughing that looked like an artillery range.) Stubble-ploughing is fairly easy too, for it will be broken down into a tilth for the potatoes. My strip of black-ground was straightforward at the top, but towards the river it became the steep kale ground that had so bothered Prince the year before. The horses needed firm handling to drive them straight down the slope, and at first they were startled by the stones like small cannon-balls which, dislodged by the sock of the plough, trundled down amongst their hoofs and gathered impetus all the way to the bottom. Next I tackled the Two-Acre field of stubble ; I can still hear the sound of " Leezie Lindsay " and " The Dashing White Sergeant " from the village Hall, where an evening dance was being held. If the work was rough-and-ready, at least I had the satisfaction of knowing that it was my own.

Whilst we kept, necessarily, to the traditional cropping of the district, we decided to try certain experiments, of which the chief was a heavy application of lime to the arable ground. For interest's sake I top-dressed a small corner of the rough grazing in the Bull Park. Within a year the better types of grass were beginning to prevail over the poorer, and both over the moss. A greener patch could readily be made out whenever we fed the hens on the rock behind the house. It would, I suggest, be a better form of publicity than most, for a lime company to pick out the four letters of the word " lime " on some barren hill beside a railway. The carrying-capacity of some stretches of hill has been enormously increased by liming, discing and re-seeding ; for our part we had to be content to concentrate on the arable.

The cost would be heavy, but if we left the farm we should recover the residual values from the next tenant, and half the cost of material and transport was borne by the Government in any case. The lime subsidy appears to me one of the wiser forms of Government aid to farmers, and there was a particularly good variant of it. At various points on the West Coast there are beautiful bays of white coral sand, which is almost pure calcium carbonate. Since the grains are fairly large and offer a relatively small surface to the weather, they take about twenty years to disintegrate in the soil, four or five times as long as powdered lime. The dressing must therefore be four or five times as heavy for corresponding results, but it is a long-term investment. From the crofter's standpoint coral sand has the merit of requiring little or no outlay of money. The labour required is considerable. In our case, the only suitable beach was on a tree-covered island over the water towards Plockton. Sand must be bagged, transferred to the mainland, and carted to the farm. The Lime Department was willing to pay a crofter half the estimated cost of all this work. Thus he could enter the worth of his own labour and the use of his own horse and cart, together with any money costs, such as the hire of a launch, and receive a cheque for half the total. There were, of course, reservations to prevent abuse. In general the effect of the subsidy was to help those who helped themselves. The scheme was less convenient for men on Forestry holdings, who would have to take time off from paid work in order to avail themselves of it, than for families wholly dependent on their crofts ; to the latter the arrangement could be of the utmost value.

Donald and I gathered some potato-bags, borrowed a rather old boat, and rowed out one calm January morning to investigate. There was excellent sand at the west end of the island. We filled the bags and stacked them on a whale-backed rock above high-water level. A woman was digging for razor-fish on the beach opposite, cold as the day was. We loaded a couple of bags into the boat for our hens, not daring to bring more lest the bottom should fall out of the boat, and set out for Fernaig shore. A choppy sea had risen in the meantime, but we beached without difficulty. Katey, who lives by the shore there, helped us to drag up the boat and filled us with tea and shell-fish.

We found that it was impracticable to fetch our own sand in this way. Before hiring a launch we should need to bag at least five tons, preferably more, and we could not lay hands on nearly enough bags for the purpose. Moreover, the days when the weather was suitable for going out to the island were too much in demand for other work. At length D. and I decided to order coral sand from a contractor farther along the coast who could deliver it by lorry at a reasonable cost.

That first spring we gave all our ploughed ground a heavy dressing except the potato-ground ; about four tons to the acre of coral sand, with a ton of Buxton powdered limestone for a quicker start. Spreading the powdered lime was gritty work on the calmest day. I always finished looking like a miller and Prince might have been any colour. It was also tiring work as it had to be done after the ploughing owing to the tendency of lime to sink into the ground. I took a good deal of trouble to spread the lime evenly, for inequalities would set up a vicious spiral of unequal grazing and unequal dunging. A machine might have done a better job ; of the implements available I found D.'s kitchen shovel the quickest. In our second and third springs at Achbeg we took a shorter view, applying three tons of powdered lime only to the acre. Most of the arable land had been treated before we left.

Lime helps to reduce the sourness of peaty soil, but its main effect is physical rather than directly chemical. It alters the texture of the soil, making it lighter, warmer, and better able to retain moisture without becoming water-logged. Our soil responded well. Visitors who viewed the farm later on as intending applicants for the tenancy were unlikely to over-praise crops they might have to purchase at valuation, and we were inclined therefore to accept their compliments at face value. Several of them admitted that they had never seen better crops on the West, and one went further than that. Potatoes showed a tendency to form wrinkled scars from the second-year lime, but neither flavour nor keeping-quality appeared to be impaired. Perhaps I may add here that I am fully aware that it takes more than a few good crops to make a farmer. The crops must be converted into livestock and the livestock into a livelihood for a family over a period of years before one can begin to claim success. We did not stay long enough to show that our methods paid. We lived, and we left the ground better than we found it ; that is all that can usefully be said. Capital gains and losses over a short period are too hard to separate from current gains and losses, and in crofting conditions— where, for example, so much labour is voluntary and unpaid—costings have too little meaning, for any definite conclusion to be drawn from our books. We formed the opinion that, so long as prices remain steady, it is possible to make a humble living with great non-monetary compensations, but that anyone wishing to save money will do better in paid employment.

We experimented also with improved strains of grasses. One is apt to think of grass as the vegetation that creeps into the gaps between crops, but (as I have said) it is itself by far the most valuable of all crops. The seed is so dear that many farmers are tempted to sow barn-floor sweepings, and the temptation is greatest on a croft. Some sort of first-year crop is obtained in return for no outlay. It is usually, however, a thin, weedy crop, and there is no means of controlling the balance of different species. One might unwittingly sow almost pure Italian rye-grass, which is an annual, and the subsequent crops would then consist only of wind-sown grass from outside. For a grass crop is normally expected to last several or many years, according to circumstances. The snag is that the ley always tends to revert to its natural condition as extraneous grasses creep in. Good management and the choice of the right seeds mixture for the particular purpose can do much to slow down the reversion, without actually preventing it. Some farmers like complex mixtures, with a pinch of this and a sprinkling of that, but fairly simple mixtures are on the whole preferred now. Research has already borne remarkable results. There are actually greater variations between different strains that have been bred within some species than between different species—variations in winter-greenness, early and late growth, resistance to frost, leafiness, yield, persistence and other qualities. It is not sufficient, therefore, to buy cocksfoot, perennial rye-grass or wild white clover ; one must specify particular strains of each. It seemed to us (and the outcome justified the calculation) that we might in the long run save money by sowing better seed. We chose a mixture recommended by Sir George Stapledon and William Davies in their book *Ley Farming*, and tried to obtain the required Aberystwith strains. I wrote to a number of firms and saw a number of agents, and found them anxious to press all kinds of unwarranted fancy grasses on anyone fool enough to buy them at fancy prices. An English firm was able to supply the mixture we wanted, and in due course the bag arrived at the station.

We tried the grass out first in the Middle Park. Apart from a number of patches of weeds, where scruans had killed the grass entirely, the vegetation here consisted almost wholly of clover ; probably too-early spring grazing had enabled the clovers to suffocate the other species. The cattle scoured whenever we put them on it. When the tractor was doing the other ploughing, therefore, we also had this field ploughed with the intention of sowing it straight back to grass. The ground was given its dressing of lime and—slag being unobtainable— a little superphosphate, and then I set about harrowing a tilth out of the upturned roots of the turf. Great care was needed to avoid scraping out lumps of turf and creating holes into which seed would vanish entirely. At first I harrowed very lightly, but in the end I had all the harrows piled one above the other and the chains following. The turves were reduced to wafers that settled into the hollows beneath them ; otherwise they would tend to dry out and kill the seedlings during the relatively dry days of spring. At last, after much waiting, the right day came—with hardly a breath of wind and a promise of rain later. Anxious to make the most of it I was out in the field before five with the fiddle, the bags of seed, bits of stick for landmarks, and a spring balance to check the progress of the seed. I sowed first lengthwise and then crosswise for safety. The may-tree, a foam of blossom up on the Face, caught the first rays of the sun, and several cuckoos were calling from the birches ; but a slight mist came up that turned gradually to a drizzle. Once the seed was in, the harrowing was simple enough in any weather, and the rain was all to the good.

Ten days later, glossy shoots began to appear, and thickened gradually into a sward. It was a healthy, deep emerald, quite different from the bluish green of sulphated grass. We rolled it with the erratic roller and gave it periodic grazing. By autumn there was a good bite on it that enabled us to delay appreciably the start of winter feeding. Next spring it came on very early. Ideally we should have grazed it then, but circumstances compelled us to take hay off it. Though it was past its most leafy stage before we could cut it, the yield was excellent—I had no means of measuring it at all accurately in tons to the acre, but it was certainly well above two. Again I will indulge myself by quoting two compliments. A local resident told us that he had always noticed what a " nasty, crabbit " field that had been, and said he would not have expected it to support such grass ; and a prospecting visitor called this the best grass he had seen in the West. Without deluding ourselves about what had been achieved, we were reassured by the bouquets. The species appeared to persist well in the third season, despite our having taken the premature crop of hay, and I hope to examine the field before the plough comes round to it again. I fear there will be a good many rashes in it, however.

In the second and third springs we did no direct re-seeding. Some of the ground seeded under corn in the ordinary rotation was sown with Aberystwith grass and some with commercial strains for comparison, but we had left before any decisive difference had emerged.

Moles gave us much trouble in the Aberystwith grass sown in the Two-Acre park. A brilliant green had come into it during March, soon hiding the dead stubble, except where laid corn had killed strips the previous autumn ; but now mounds of earth were killing small patches everywhere, so that plates of solid weed were established in the grass. I put the chains over the mounds, and at the same time rolled in all stones (to prevent trouble for the scythes later). Next day there were fresh mole-hills in dozens. I spread the new mounds daily with a graip, but the moles were winning. I had never before thought much about these odd creatures that live in a dark world under our feet. Their tunnels must flood like mole-drains in bad weather. They die in a matter of hours when they cannot find food, and eat one another in the desperation of hunger. I never cease to wonder at the endless variety of self-consistent patterns in Nature, from the mole-ness of the mole to the minute, brave squareness of the tormentil up on Ree Breac. Nor can I begin to understand the attitude of those who kill God's creatures in the effort to kill time. But there was little choice about trapping these moles. One by one we caught them, with their velvety fur, their long tapering snouts, and their pathetic, uncanny baby hands. As the cats would not look at them, we had to give them proper burial.

Our third intended experiment was with composting. Compost, like folk-art, seems to attract all kinds of querulous and bigoted people, but that is beside the point.

However united a front farmers may present to the rest of the community, the world of farmers (and gardeners) suffers fierce internal divisions of opinion, one of the chief being the artificials-compost dispute. Many books have been devoted to it ; here I can give only the briefest statement.

The case for the use of artificial manures rests on the

inoffensive proposition that you cannot take out of the soil what has not been put in. If plants require particular substances in greater quantities than a given soil supplies them, the natural thing to do is to make good the deficiency. In addition, the nitrogenous fertilisers act as a stimulant to plant life ; they are sometimes called " the alcohol of the soil." The increases in crop yields that have been achieved by the use of artificials are too well known to need description.

Those who oppose the use of artificials do so on various grounds. They point out, for instance, that the SO_4 ion of sulphate of ammonia accumulates indefinitely to poison the soil. Essentially their case is that what goes on in the soil is vastly more complex than a merely arithmetical view would suggest. There is a vast amount of organic activity in the soil, they maintain, which is slowed down or even stopped by the use of artificials. There is an intermediate stage in the absorption of minerals into plants that depends upon the co-operation of vast numbers of fungi and bacteria. Ordinary farmyard manure is insufficient in modern conditions to maintain this complex state of fertility, and methods have therefore been devised to multiply its effect by the systematic return of all animal and vegetable wastes by composting. The Indore process is the best-known of these methods. Those who put their trust in compost assert that healthy animals (including humans) are dependent on healthy vegetable life and this in turn upon organically healthy soil conditions.

I have inevitably over-simplified both views, but there is no lack of other material available to anyone interested.

It must be admitted, on the one hand, that the assertions of the compost school often go far beyond the demonstrable facts ; but so too has many an intuitive judgment that has later proved sound. There would be nothing surprising in the discovery that a more delicate play of forces occurs in the soil than was formerly recognised. Equally it must be admitted that the record of recent prodigality in the use of the world's resources does not give one much confidence in the simple, profit-and-loss outlook of " progressive " farming. (The official *Report on the Post-War Loaf* reveals a fantastic situation. It is as though a farmer should feed his cream to his pigs and his skim milk to his family, simultaneously persuading them to pity the poor folk who have to drink whole-milk.) The truth will only be arrived at through patient, painstaking experiments like those of the Haughley Research Trust farms in Suffolk.* Meanwhile it is significant that the advertisements for artificials have retreated to the more tenable assertion that *both* humus and artificials are needed. One further point may be made, I think, without the imputation of bias. Great numbers of shareholders are dependent for their dividends on the continued use of artificials ; there is no corresponding financial interest in the application of humus.

We felt, then, D. and I, that whilst the case was definitely not proven there was ample reason for experiment on any scale. We encountered two difficulties, however. The first was that of obtaining enough vegetable matter. I made a moderate-sized heap on the Indore model, mixing seaweed and the half-decayed deciduous leaves from the bank on the shore with farmyard manure and a sprinkling of powdered lime. It heated up beautifully, according to book. When the leaves were exhausted I tried the most abundant of all waste vegetable matter in the district, the rashes. But their stiffness kept the heap too airy and their outer peel proved highly resistant to decomposition. The heap stood for months without visible change, though it ultimately broke down into a poor type of humus. Bracken always seemed to shrink to nothing and iris-leaves had the same faults as rashes. The other difficulty was the amount of labour required to build and turn the heaps without mechanised help. Either difficulty alone might have been surmounted in the end, but, when there was so much else to think about, the two together defeated us. We reverted to the rough composting that is traditional along the

* An admirable account is given in *The Living Soil*, by Lady Eve Balfour.

Western shore, the layering of seaweed and muck on the midden.

The first and most successful heap broke down into a crumbling black substance about which one could easily get sentimental. We gave it a rough trial on the potato-field. One-third of the ground was dunged before the ploughing; a second section was dunged in the drill; and the third was dressed with humus applied direct in the drill. We also sowed a transverse strip with a heavier application of artificial. Of course we expected no very definite results from a single application, but we were a little surprised by the sequel. The six different types of treatment showed not the slightest perceptible difference in the crop.

It is common to top-dress grass with sulphate at a hundredweight to the acre early in the season, and sometimes also a little before cutting-time. At first we tried this on our meadow-hay, and there is no doubt about the short-term results. We came to suspect, however, that on such poor soil stimulation of this kind led to rapid depletion that was not counteracted by liming or top-dressing with dung or both. There is only a narrow reserve of fertility in the Highland soil. In a field of (commercial) seeds hay, I sowed one part only with sulphate. By whatever process, the balance of herbage was disturbed in the section dressed, and it was possible to see next year exactly where the sulphate had been sown by the almost complete lack of clover. On a field of Donald's there was an equally striking demonstration. Nothing could safely be deduced from such slender evidence, but we came to rely less and less upon sulphate, and never applied it to the Aberystwith grass. The other artificial usually applied in the district is ready-mixed potato manure, euphemistically known as " guano." Excessive applications make the potatoes watery, but we formed no opinion on the efficacy of lighter dressings.

A well-meaning man with a pipe called one evening to inspect our cattle. On seeing the electric fence he inferred

that I was a " College man," and confided his belief that
nobody round about was interested in farming—this in a
Glen where many of the men run a croft more or less in
their spare time from work in the Forestry. He looked
with approval at the Aberystwith grass in the stubble
across the road and told me that if I would lime it at a
ton to the acre and apply 1½ cwt. of sulphate I should
get a good crop from it. I assured him that I had already
limed it at several tons to the acre and that nothing would
persuade me to risk sulphate or nitro-chalk on it just then.
I showed him the line between clover and no-clover in
the other grass, and he confessed himself puzzled. He was
surprised to hear of our eighty inches of rain and our
run-down, washed-out soil. On some matters I valued
his advice, and I have a great regard for most officials on
their own ground ; but his attitude was not calculated to
bridge the gap that unfortunately exists between West-
Coast farmers and Edinburgh officials.

Much the same contrast was vividly shown during one
of our visits to market. The wind that had disrupted our
stack had broken one of the trams of Gordon's cart, and
we went along to see the smith about metal strips for
repairing it. The smithy was a marvel of order in seeming
disorder. From the ceiling and all the walls dangled
strings of washers, bundles of shoes, stocks and dies, tools,
materials, and I don't know what else. Of the rows upon
rows of little drawers no two seemed to have similar
handles and none had labels. But the floor was clear, and
the smith's hand found whatever he needed without hesitation. He listened quietly to Gordon, his manner neither
servile nor off-hand. He started to make the strips and I
imagined that all his attention was on his work, but he
called across to a soldier who was shoeing a grey horse
that it was dangerous to go *under* this particular animal.
He chalked his memos on the cowl of the forge. Not
having suitable bolts he said that he would make them
and send a boy along with them to our train—and did.
He was master of his own ground and at home. From

there we went to visit an official in his little office. Stacks of dreary papers, sordid furniture, straw-board walls, and a stolid, unblinking electric fire under the table. The official, we found, knew his job quite as well as the black-smith ; his materials were as readily to hand and his work as important ; yet there was a gulf between the two men, and between their respective worlds. I asked my com-panions which they would rather be, and they all said, the blacksmith.

To return to our experiments, there were two others that were definite failures. The first was the sowing of broadcast kale. It is said to give at least an equal yield for less trouble. The piece of ground on which I tried it happened to be particularly " dirty " ground. Once the kale was up, no hoeing or harrowing was possible. For a little while the kale plants went ahead ; but all too soon the spurrey and other weeds caught up on them, and in the end it was hard to find a kale plant in the riot of weeds. We turned the cows on to this patch and they devoured everything, spurrey, kale and all.

Finally, there was the good intention of making grass silage. We aimed at getting our hay in early, during the finer weather of June and July, and the aftermath could then be cut for silage in the late autumn. I began to dig a pit at what seemed a suitable spot, but came across living rock when the pit was well advanced. Blasting would demolish the whole pit and there was no time to start afresh elsewhere. I therefore chipped away at the rock until the weather broke. When at last the weather cleared, it was too late in the season and we put the tups on the foggage. Next year there was a different obstacle : there was for a while a possibility that we might be leaving at the Michaelmas Term. An incoming tenant was obliged to buy standing crops and would probably buy our stacks as an act of grace, but he might well refuse to take over a pit of silage. Nothing ever went into the pit, therefore —nothing except two hedgehogs which we found there in the spring. They had, I suspect, found a fine and private place, but had been trapped without water. One died and the other was with difficulty revived. My imagination recoils before the thought of the loves of the hedgehog, and I should like to have been a witness.

The advertised tenancy brought in enquiries from places as remote as Lerwick in Shetland and Berwick on the Border. A good many people came to see over the farm, including some who hardly knew a sheep from a goat. (We learned that farm-visiting is a recognised entertainment.) Two complaints were common, that the rent was too high and the house too small. The former I could readily understand. It is true that many persons elsewhere pay for a single room several times the rent we paid for two hundred acres with the house and outbuildings thrown in ; but then they don't have to pay it in calves and lambs. At the same time, the rent could hardly have been less. When upkeep and depreciation had been allowed for on the buildings, miles of fences and other " improvements," I believe the rent in the economic sense may well have been less than nothing. Farms under the Forestry comprise the less plantable ground that has had to be bought, and their policy may be to minimise their loss rather than to make an actual gain. The second complaint is interesting. Houses for the poor have long (and rightly) been subsidised out of the incomes of the rich ; but as subsidised houses grow more numerous and as the disparity between incomes grows less, we are approaching the theoretically possible state in which everyone pays part of everyone else's rent. The net effect has been a rise in the standard of housing expected (which is good), and the disappearance of any notion of cutting the coat according to the cloth (which is bad). The house at Achbeg would be a tight fit for a family of any considerable size ; but a person who seeks to get a living out of nineteen acres of poor arable and two hundred of inferior hill ground cannot expect to live in a mansion. Compared with the rows of match-boxes for which there are now long waiting-lists, Achbeg house, with its solid walls, its two good living-rooms, and its plot of garden,

if not a mansion, was in its humble way a very adequate
home and castle. D. and I happened to need little house-
room, but some pretty large families had been brought up
in the house before our time, without, as far as we ever
heard, any sense of grievance.

A Shetland family, from the northernmost part of
Unst, the northernmost of all the British islands, midway
between the Border and the Arctic Circle, accepted the
tenancy. Most visitors remarked upon our isolation at
Achbeg, but to our successors the Glen was almost urban.
The children, though familiar with aeroplanes, had never
seen a train before. Surprisingly the Shetland accent has
affinities with broad Scots rather than with the English of
the Highlands ; Gaelic of course is not spoken in the
Shetlands.

We worked out agreed prices for the stock and crops
privately instead of by valuation, and saved ourselves the
fee. There had to be a full gathering of sheep for the
inspection of the count. Two ewes with their lambs gave
us more trouble than the rest put together. They had
discovered the luscious grass in the Forestry at Ardnarff
several miles away. Every now and then they would be
spotted in a clearing, or word would come that they were
in mortal danger on the line, but to get them out was a
considerable undertaking. At length Donald and I, with
his dog Prince, surprised them and forced them on to the
line. We raced them along to Strome, for a train was due,
mixed them with others, and put them in the most stock-
proof of the parks. Two mornings later they had gone,
lambs and all. They were soon reported back on the old
spot. We made another attempt to get them out, but they
were off at top speed along the fire-track and we could
find no trace of them. We went home, and there they
were up above the Face, having bolted the whole distance
back on to our hill. Very cautiously we closed in on them
and brought them down to the steading. The count being
due next day, we kept them in overnight to give them no
opportunity at all. But I have little doubt they were back

N

at Ardnarff within a day or two, and we told the new tenant where to expect them. There were no better lambs in the flock, such is the grass at Ardnarff.

As the byre began to look empty and the time came for making our round of farewells, we discovered how deep our roots had gone at Achbeg. We should miss such kindly neighbours. It is the custom to scrub-out the whole house completely at a Highland flitting. All this and much of the packing were done for us by them unasked, and those who could not come over sent scones and other food to save D. the need for cooking. A number of them came down to the early morning train to see us off. We watched the receding houses by the loch and the diminishing bulk of Achbeg hill, no longer " our " hill, and said that in one way or another we must certainly return.

CHAPTER XII

SOCIAL COHERENCE

" And how like you this shepherd's life, Master Touchstone ? "
. . . As it is a spare life, look you, it fits my humour well ; but as
there is no more plenty in it, it goes much against my stomach.
Hast any philosophy in thee, shepherd ? "

SHAKESPEARE—" As You Like It."

And now it is chalk-dust once more that collects in the
corners of my pockets, instead of hayseed, and the sheep
bleating in the night keep somebody else awake. Teaching
has its satisfactions—the satisfactions of watching the timid
acquire confidence, the aggressive outgrow their aggression, and the irresponsible take on responsibility. They
are deep and lasting, but seldom immediate. There is no
pleasure in teaching like that of a certain midgy summer
evening at Achbeg. I stood on the rock in the steading
looking across at the Two-Acre Park. A slight yellow-
ness was creeping into the translucent green of the corn,
sign that in a few days it would be ready for the scythe.
With Prince and Dicky I had ploughed that ground ; with
Donald I had sown it ; with my neighbours I should soon
be cutting it and stooking it and rattling it into the barn
between showers. It had responded well to the lime and
seemed to me a good crop : plenty of head for the hens
and straw to see Prince and the cows over Christmas.
The weather might beat us yet ; and in other circumstances
Danish eggs and Argentine beef might have knocked the
meaning out of it all ; but there it stood quietly ripening
with the ring of dark conifers behind and closer the rashes
that resume possession of any unworked fields in the district. The outcome of effort is never so immediate nor so
tangible in education. Perhaps some day we should have
returned to crofting ; it is easy to imagine conditions in

which honest teaching would be impossible, but for as long as Britain is a free country the need for teachers will be at least equal to the need for crofters.

Looking back, I am inclined to sentimentalise, allowing memory to sieve the realities. Acres of sea-pinks flash before my mind's eye when I recall our years in the North : the sea-pinks of the Island, and whole fields of daisies there folding from white to rose at dusk ; the frozen lochans on Ree Breac ; ducklings ; the calf Noel with upturned bucket on his head, like a knight in a small-town pageant ; briars in bud, in leaf, in flower, in berry, and in the thorny bareness of winter ; the gloss on the Aberystwith grass in sunshine ; the wonderful clean bareness of the stubble-field, cleared at last, and the smiles round the kitchen table. I hear the first piping of the year's first lamb, and the abrupt silence in the hollows on windy days ; the shameless greed of the cattle on winter evenings ; the hiss and crackle and snarl of burning heather ; "Fiunary" in a high tenor voice ; the rattle of the door-handle that announced letters from outside. And it is not only for the eye and the ear that memory has pleasures. There is the tang of seaweed ; the seasonal scents of primroses, bluebells, mown hay, sheep packed tight in the gripping-pen, heather in bloom and heather burning ; and the stimulating odours of the long days putting out muck. And I can feel now the tingle of corn from under the stick, and the exhilaration of the south-wester on the shore. How Prince hated it. All these are stored, ready for the slightest beck of memory.

Others no less authentic do not leap to mind so eagerly. There was the aching vastness of weedy potato-drills, or of spread hay with a shower racing in from Applecross ; the worry of March and April as the stacks dwindled and still the grass showed no sprout of new green ; the sordid Sunday cackle of the hens ; the trickle down the spine and the squelch of feet in leaky boots ; the endless drizzle as the grass went to stem and seed ; there was maggot, that living death ; the weeks of painful waiting for the dentist ; war-time whisky ; and the midges, the petty, crawling, stabbing, insignificant, insufferable multitudes of midges.

Pleasant and unpleasant, these are mostly small things; and if small things—the links in the chain of life—have their importance they must yield to the big things. What appealed to us was more than the sum-total of these, it was the feeling of the life as a whole. For all its limitations and shortcomings, it was a good life, a coherent, meaningful, *human* way of living. The contrast between newer and older modes was epitomised in a small incident. A long-distance bus in which D. and I were travelling flashed past a roadside group, an old crofter and his wife, staring miserably at a cow in a deep ditch. There were men on the bus who could easily have lifted out the cow; but no, it never slackened speed. The time-table to which the driver was clamped made no allowance for such humanities and we never knew the cow's fate. Without the bus, its time-table, and its background of machinery and appointments, it is true, our journey would have been impossible; but impossible, unthinkable too would have been the withholding of a neighbourly hand. We had few of the advantages of the machine world in the Glen, but we had in abundance the greater blessing of neighbourliness. Our life was geared, not to an arbitrary schedule, but to the weather and the process of the seasons. It was simple, even hard, but it was right. In spite of the shadow of the city, in spite of the subsidies, and in spite of our own grumbling and the contempt of passing hikers, it was a good life.

This topic, the contrast between the ways of the Glen and the ways of the outside world, was the subject of many, many discussions. By our fireside D. and I often argued about it with Donald into the small hours. When jolting home by moonlight after a day with the horses "up the Glen," or when picking our way along a path tinkling with ice-crystals to burn heather on Ree Breac, and once on a sharp ledge of the Face when rain caught us after we had dressed a sick wedder, Donald and I debated it without end, until each came near to convincing the other. There was no gainsaying Donald's main contention that the Highlanders have been shamefully ill-treated from the time of the evictions onward. Highland farming is therefore not typical of peasant farming, nor was our experience typical of Highland farming. Thus I cannot presume to offer any " conclusions " arising from our few years in the North, but there is this central reflection on the coherence and meaningfulness of life in the Glen as compared with more " modern " ways of living. Perhaps I may be permitted, before taking my leave of the reader, to underline that contrast, to make explicit what is, I believe, implicit in the foregoing narrative.

We had very little capital equipment to assist us in the Glen—no thresher, no binder, no permanent tractor even ; still less had we fantastically expensive and exacting equipment like a modern continuous-strip mill. Whatever the losses, there was at least one gain from the system, that we were freer in planning our lives. When workers clock-in for the night shift at a big factory, it is not because anyone likes clocking-in or the reversal of night and day, but because their tools impose these conditions of work. That is the price that must be paid for increased production. Our production was low ; but (apart from the dependence on the whims of the market) we always felt that our fate was in our own hands. Our lives were a tissue of big and small decisions, of real responsibilities, or tasks which, if they were not so diverse as invariably to have immediate interest, were never without meaning. And, living in such a world, D. and I became more clearly aware of certain contrasting dangers of the more modern world. They arise from the concentration and specialisation that necessarily accompany the use of machinery. You can specialise techniques to any point, but you cannot specialise human nature indefinitely ; beyond some point the salt of life breaks down into dangerous elements.

First, we were our own employers in the Glen. In all but a few professions—farming, jobbing-building and shop-keeping*—the employers are usually separate individuals from the employees. Consequently all sorts of elaborate checks and counterchecks are needed—comparative costings, time cards, automatic logs, the conveyor-belt and others—to make sure that the workers do not cheat the employers. They are an insult to the integrity of the workers, but they are absolutely necessary *in a system that differentiates workers from employers* (or managers). A system that openly humiliates most members of the community is patently a vicious system. But within the family, at the other extreme, there is little thought of mutual evasion and cheating, and the family is therefore the ideal economic unit. Seldom, except on a croft, can that ideal be attained. On a croft there is no need for elaborate checks and incentives. Gordon used to tell a story of a friend of his bothy days. After long saving and expectation the friend decided to take a small farm of his own. " There will be no more rising at five and jumping around at the grieve's command for me," he said gleefully to Gordon in a Doric I will not try to reproduce. A few months later Gordon enquired how the new scheme was working. " Man, man," said the friend, " I never worked for a harder master. He's never away from my elbow." But he wasn't complaining, and wouldn't think of returning to the relative security of a farm-servant's wage. Gordon himself has just taken the same courageous plunge.

The self-employed worker has the perfect boss, whose eye misses nothing but who never fails in sympathy. Circumstances set the problem : given the Highland soil and climate, for instance, and the conditions generally, make a living for yourself and your family by what means you will. There is no knocker-up and no starting hooter ; equally there is none for knocking-off. At every stage of the day the man himself must balance (say) the pleasure of a quiet pipe in the shelter of the dyke against the need for cutting an extra swathe of bedding. He and his family

* And, most important of all, housekeeping ; but since housewives add nothing to that curious abstraction the national income, their work is usually assumed to be unproductive.

must judge the day's weather, and cope with the wet corn if they misjudge. They must decide whether to keep the black calf and sell the roan, or sell them both ; whether to grade the blue-grey or make a sucker of her ; whether to keep to Rhode Islands or to try out other breeds, or even geese, ducks and turkeys ; just what to sow, and when. They must decide to the best of their ability, and bear the consequences. There is nothing to gain from skimped work, but equally there is nothing furtive in relaxation ; and when things go wrong there is no resentment against the decisions of a higher authority since the weather is beyond human control. One has to have worked in such conditions to apprehend the full ugliness of the term " industrial discipline."

Second, we consumed much of our own produce in the Glen, and obtained many of our own raw materials, so that the relation between effort and reward was self-evident. Where the producer and the consumer are separate individuals or groups, specialisation sets one part of the community against another—the farmer against the housewife, the Lancashire mill-girl against a foreign competitor. Moreover, in a money economy it is not always the most admirable qualities that are the most advantageous. A good line of talk, a thick skin, unlimited push, and a keen eye for a bargain have their value in commerce : they make very little impression on a field of turnips. Even crofting is now a compromise, for buying and selling play an increasing part in it. Like any other self-employed persons we had to think and talk much of prices—visitors said we talked of nothing else. One can, I imagine, reach a stage where a calf is nothing but a five-pound note on legs, and a field of clover nothing but the difference between two lamb-cheques. Matters do not go so far on a croft : when the old brown cow, whose milk has fed all the babies in their turn, finally goes off to market, there is usually a terrible wailing in the family, and I recall a crofter who, when selling his horse, rejected a higher price for a better home for the animal.

At least we had not the humiliating knowledge of utter
dependence on others. Whereas the specialised worker
must sell his goods or services to others whom he cannot
oblige to want them, and if he fails to sell them is cut off
from all the necessities of life, the crofter can always fall
back on his own resources. Children from an early age
helped willingly in the fields in the Glen, and especially
in the tending of the animals, because they knew already
the full significance of each particular action. Not only
has every operation in crofting its reason : it has an
obvious reason, a reason patent to all concerned, and one
in no way arbitrary. No system of production targets in
a planned economy or of private gain in a competitive
economy could be a substitute for the self-explanatory
quality and the independence of the crofting life.

Third, machinery had not been allowed in the Glen to
divide leisure from work. There are on a croft spells of
pure work and spells of pure leisure, but no clear line of
demarcation is drawn by any wage-agreement between
" the firm's time " and God's. When Donald helped us
until midnight to put in some threatened hay, I am quite
certain that he made no overtime entry in a mental time-
sheet. Again, the hours that I spent taking Marie to the
bull counted as work as the journey *had* to be made, but
I spend much of my leisure in just this fashion ; and the
many hours we spent reading and talking of farming
matters—I should not care to have to enter them on a
costings analysis.

Finally, our work was varied. There were the sheep,
the cattle and the poultry to consider ; the hill-work and
the arable ; from the rush of the spring-work to the comparative relaxation of winter, every season brought new
tasks. And the planning and co-ordination of these tasks
offered plenty to keep the mind occupied. Moreover we
all shared in all the operations, from the selection of stock
and other such decisions down to the " tattie-hooking."
In a more modern community, not only is a given worker's
job specialised into inanity (putting the crosses on a million

hot-cross buns, for instance), but all the functions that give meaning and dignity to life—the designing, the planning, the making of decisions—are being concentrated in the hands of a small class of persons. This class is self-perpetuating. In Britain our school system picks out the brightest pupils and gives them a special training; they marry within their class; and the new hereditary stratification of society, into the managers and the managed, holds a greater threat to human happiness than any of the past. Freedom without responsibility is a negative concept, and the whole trend of " specialist " society is towards the concentration of responsibility rather than its diffusion.

These, then, were four aspects of specialisation that had as yet hardly affected the Glen—the divorce of employer from worker, of producer from consumer, of leisure from work, and of responsibility from execution. What is disturbing is that all these effects are not incidental to machine technique, but intimately and essentially a part of specialisation, which is inseparable from machine technique. The main outcome, therefore, of our experiences in the Glen was the strengthening of our doubt as to the possibility of a leisure civilisation. Where work is creative, leisure also is creatively employed. In a previous chapter I have said something on the quality of Highland leisure activities; but they presuppose a society in which each man's work offers grounds for self-respect and encourages the development of personality. In the promised leisure civilisation of the future, it is the spare-time activities that must be the source of self-respect and of personal fulfilment. To Keats it was, admittedly, his poetry that gave meaning to life, and that has always been the case for a favoured, intelligent minority; the undiscussed assumption made by those who look forward to a leisure civilisation based on the machine is that what was possible to Keats is possible to everyone—the butcher, the baker, the candle-stick-maker. All the evidence of history goes against that assumption. Even to-day, if a man earns money as a mechanic purely in order that he may devote his private

energies to playing the fiddle, nobody will say that he " is "
a fiddler : he " is " a mechanic. In the future, what has
always been the tail must learn to wag the dog. The
obvious danger is that we shall achieve, not a new freedom, but a new variant of the old formula of bread and
circuses. Already there are sinister indications. Expenditure on alcohol and tobacco came close behind expenditure
on food during the recent war, and at the very worst
period sailors continued to give their lives in order that
the supply of narcotics should be maintained. Every
wage-earner at present devotes, on an average, ten shillings
a week to gambling ; and the Government in order to
stimulate effort in the minefields sends in not more teachers
for the miners' children, or more books and music for
their leisure, but more nylon stockings.

In short, it is plain that the shift from a more primitive
life such as that of the Highlands to that of large-scale
industry has set the world problems much deeper than the
monotony of work, the fortuitous badness of design, the
slum, and personal exploitation. Better planning could
end all these and still leave the life of man nasty, brutish
and long ; it could still leave us with no sense of belonging
and no sense of fulfilment. The problem is to restore a
sense of the coherence and rationality of our community
life, the feeling that our fate is in our own hands. I well
remember an evening during the time of acute national
fuel shortage, spent by a neighbour's fireside in the Glen.
Despite the bitter cold outside, the kitchen was almost too
warm. The blazing logs had been cut and split that afternoon by my host and his wife—slow, heavy work, but
within their own control. Wanting a brighter fire they
had only to cut more wood. It was possible to say to a
boy there, " You may have a fire in your room whenever
you wish—provided you cut the wood yourself." Logically
it might be the same to say : " If you can find some way
of earning sixpence, I will let you have six-pennyworth of
coal for your fire," but psychologically there is the difference between bread and a stone.

It is partly a question of scale, of mere size. Ideally the economic unit would (as I have suggested) be the social unit, the family. It can safely be expanded just so long as it is *felt* to be coherent ; so long as each person's function in relation to the others' is self-evident. Such was the condition of the semi-independent village community. Such still is the crofting township. But now for most of us the effective community is the two billion inhabitants of the globe, which means no community at all. It is commonly said that the great threat to our continued existence arises from the fact that the economic unit has outgrown the governmental unit ; there is the further possibility that both have outgrown the social unit. If that is so, the remedy does not lie in trying to change human nature.

There may be much significance in the present job-and-an-acre trend in America ; for food-growing as a leisure activity is different from most others. To spend fifty hours of leisure making a chair by hand when a single hour at the machine will produce one that is perfectly serviceable will always seem rather dilettante to most people ; and music, painting and so on are unlikely to absorb sufficient energy. Food-growing, however, combines the satisfaction of creative instincts with immediate utility. Fresh, home-grown food has demonstrable advantages over bought food in almost any economy. In essentials, the movement resembles that for the provision of Forestry holdings (though the Forestry Commission is unhappily reversing its policy, providing now houses which have not even a decent garden), in that it aims to provide the best of both worlds—to combine (on the worker's side) an assured income with some of the advantages of the freeholder. Perhaps a compromise with the machine will be worked out along some such lines. There are machines which hold the family unit together rather than drive it apart (and from my experience as a teacher I can foresee no tolerable future that entails the breakdown of the family) ; the sewing-machine, for instance, the washing-machine, and possibly the rototiller. In Britain also there is a move to decentralise industry ; a few light industries may even reach the electrified Highland glens. Thus it is conceivable that the future may see along with the development of industry a complementary growth of part-time holdings. Something of the satisfaction of crofting might then be more widely available—the variety of work, the co-operation with natural forces, the struggle with the weather, the sense of difficulty overcome, the intimate acquaintance with wild creatures and with natural beauty, the mutual help of neighbours, probably too a limited feeling of community—all these and more might be possible. Not all people will want holdings, but I believe there are wider possibilities in this direction than in a concentration on non-utilitarian arts and crafts.

There is, however, one important difference between Forestry holdings and true crofts that may help us to keep perspective. Whereas a competent crofter has absolute security of tenure, the Forestry worker is subject to a month's notice to quit. Inevitably so. Just how deep is the opposition between freedom and industrialism was brought out in one of the most interesting chapters of recent Scottish history, Lord Leverhulme's attempt to modernise the island of Lewis. Mr Colin Macdonald, who has devoted his life to the cause of Highland farming, gives an account of the venture in his delightful book *Highland Journey*. Leverhulme bought the island after the first World War and prepared to sink five million pounds into bringing it prosperity. There were to be spotting aeroplanes, a perfectly equipped herring fleet, huge canneries at Stornoway, rapid carrier vessels for the fresh fish, a chain of corner stores, and a vast advertising campaign. Nothing was omitted : he arranged even to control the railway in order to prevent delays. The Lewismen newly home from the war were interested enough in his schemes, but to them the independence of a croft was the first concern. They wanted land ; Leverhulme would not give them it. There were land raids and at length a large meeting was called at which Leverhulme explained his scheme. He believed that it would bring such prosperity that crofts would soon be vacant without a bidder. At the meeting a crofter-fisherman, speaking very slowly in a strong Lewis accent, made this remarkable speech :

"Lord Leverhulme, will you allow me to intervene in this debate for a few moments ? " (Assent signified.) "Thank you. Well, I will begin by saying that we give credit to your lordship for good *intentions* in this matter. We believe you *think* you are *right*, but we *know* that you are *wrong*. The fact is, there is an element of sentiment in the situation which it is impossible for your lordship to understand. But for that we do not blame you ; it is not your *fault* but your *misfortune* that your upbringing, your experience, and your outlook are ..ch that a proper understanding of the position and of our point of view is quite outwith your comprehension. You have spoken of steady work and steady pay in tones of veneration—and I have no doubt that ir. ˙ ˎ ır view, and in the view of those unfortunate people who are compelled to live their lives in smoky towns, steady work and steady pay are very desirable things. But in Lewis we have never been accustomed to either—and, strange though it must seem to your lordship, *we do not greatly desire them*. We attend to our crofts in seed-time and harve˙ ˙ and we follow the fishing in its season— and when neither requi. ˓s our attention we are free to *rest and contemplate*. You have referred to our houses as hovels—but they are our *homes*, and I will venture to say, my lord, that, poor though these homes may be, you will find more *real human happiness* in them than you will find in your *castles* throughout the land. I would impress on you that we are not in opposition to your schemes of work ; we only oppose you when you say you *cannot give us the land*, and on that point we will oppose you with all our strength. It may be that some of the younger and less thoughtful men will side with you, but believe me, the great majority of us are against you.

"Lord Leverhulme ! You have bought this island. But you have not bought *us*, and we refuse to be the bond-slaves of any man. We want to live our own lives in our own way, poor in material things it may be, but at least it will be clear of the fear of the factory bell ; it will be *free and independent* ! "

Later, Mr. Macdonald urged Leverhulme to compromise. After evasions Leverhulme finally stated the real issue. "But I *must* have control of my factory hands ! How can I have that in the case of men who are in the independent position of crofters ? I will *not* compromise. I *must* control," he reiterated !

On this rock Leverhulme's venture foundered. He left for the mainland, having first (we were told) made generous provision for those who had opposed him. An experiment that might almost have had the sharpness of a laboratory demonstration thus ended inconclusively. Would the Lewismen ultimately have accepted the prosperity offered them? One wonders what would have happened in the slump of ten years later; and one wonders whether they would ever have come to terms with that crucial " I *must* control."

The manager, whether elected or nominated, *must* control; that is his business. No part-time holding therefore will carry a secure tenure, and it will never give the degree of independence that is the crofter's chief asset. Perhaps the attempt to get the best of both worlds is really an attempt to serve both God and Mammon; perhaps at some time a conscious choice will have to be made between more prosperity and more freedom. There is little doubt about the immediate future. The world is off on a logarithmic curve of material consumption and the impulse will have to run its course. Only a few of the young people who left the Highlands during the war are keen to go back. But an increasing number of men and women who have tasted the pleasures of the industrial world and have found them largely dust in the mouth are turning to the harder, simpler life of farming. Though the crofting system itself may belong to a world that will never return, it embodies values that have been ignored at heavy cost. Sooner or later they will regain their hold. In the game of progress there are snakes as well as ladders, and it is a game which, we trust, has hardly begun.

Postscript to the second edition

At least two people are needed to run a croft. At Achbeg the second person was my wife Dorothy. She was a white South African, and had been somewhat lamed from birth by polio. She believed that nothing could harm you if you were not afraid of it, and she would swim unharmed among the sharks in Table Bay; later she spent her summers exploring the Italian hill-towns, quite unaccompanied, though there were brigands in the hills and murders were not uncommon.

We returned from our crofting to Devon, where my teaching job had been kept open for me, and our rented house was still available, when Dorothy was struck down by an utterly unforeseen brain haemorrhage. She was taken to the district Cottage Hospital, where the doctors made a lumbar puncture that for a while took away most of the pain, which had been unimaginably severe. At one point Dorothy asked me if I thought that the pain might return, and I could see that there was fear in her eyes. The pain did return, and Dorothy died. The hospital staff were astonishingly kind but of course they were essentially powerless to help.